Pat Tillman

He Graduated Life With Honors and No Regrets

By Rich Wolfe

Published by Lone Wolfe Press

ISBN: 0-9729249-7-3

Cover Photo: Dick Fox
Cover Design: Dick Fox
Photo Editor: Dick Fox
Cover Copywriter: Dick Fox
Interior Design: The Printed Page, Phoenix, AZ

The author, Rich Wolfe, can be reached at 602-738-5889 or at www.fandemonium.net.

Publishers Note: The page count expanded from 161 to 185 to reflect the number of full page photos in this book.

DEDICATION

To all the men and women who have ever
served in the United States Military.

ACKNOWLEDGMENTS

Compiling the material for *Pat Tillman—He Graduated Life with Honors and No Regrets* has been an experience I shall never forget. During this difficult time, his friends, teammates and coaches have opened their hearts to tell their personal experiences—the fun, excitement and interesting times spent with the amazing Pat Tillman.

Sincere thanks to Rich Martinez at the *San Jose Mercury News*, Jim Ripley and C. J. Cippola at the *East Valley Tribune*, Debbie Brazier in Davenport, the *Chicago Sun-Times*, Matt Storin old cohorts at the *Boston Globe*, the *Los Angeles Times*, old Dakota pal Al Neuharth and the Sage of New London, Ron "Whitey" Parsons.

This book would not have been possible without the considerable efforts of sexy Bob Jacobsen, the talented Scott Bordow, Matt Fulks, the chief in Kansas City and Travis Seibert Foxx. Nothing is possible without Barbara Jane Bookman, the Belle of Louisville and how about Steve Selby in Memphis?

A tip of the hat to the late Steve Merhtens and George Bodenheimer at ESPN, Congressman Jim Leach and Sheila Deluhery in Washington, and Barrister Crawford Shaw who keeps us on the straight and narrow, while being a blast at the same time.

Let us not forget the extra efforts of Ellen Brewer in Edmond, OK and the knock-down gorgeous Carol Reddy. Special thanks to Lisa Liddy, The Printed Page, Phoenix, AZ, for her hard work at all hours of the day and night, and her patience and professionalism in pulling the many pieces of this book together.

PREFACE

"I wonder where Pat Tillman is?" It was just a passing thought, said aloud to no one in particular as the F-15s flew over 600,000 people at the Esplanade in Boston last Fourth of July. If you like patriotic music, fireworks and the Fourth of July, there is no better place in America than with the Boston Pops on the Charles River celebrating Independence Day in the Cradle of Liberty. It is one of those rare occasions that will send shivers up your spine and a tear down your cheek.

Two weeks later, in Los Angeles for the annual ESPY awards, a friend, who was also in Boston for the Fourth said, "What was the name of that person you mentioned during the flyover?" I said, "Pat Tillman. Why?"

"He's going to be here tomorrow night to receive the Arthur Ashe Award for Courage. Who is he?"

"You're kidding! He's my favorite football player of all time if you don't count Joe Montana."

I told my friend and his wife about Tillman's exploits at Arizona State University and for the Arizona Cardinals. I was a season ticket holder for both during much of Tillman's career. The first time I saw him, I thought "Boy, Frank Kush (the retired, legendary ASU coach) would love this guy." Tillman reminded me of Ronnie Lee, my favorite NBA player ever. Lee was a first-round draft pick of the Phoenix Suns a quarter of a century ago, a lefty who couldn't throw a basketball in the Pacific Ocean from the Santa Monica Pier. But did he ever hustle! His defense was so tenacious that one night a frustrated Earl "The Pearl" Monroe slapped him. Before Lee blew out his knee, I would tell friends, "Give me five Ronnie Lees, we'll contest every game, and every fan will go away happy." Tillman was my new Ronnie Lee. He was rough and tumble, hard-hitting, spirited and aggressive without being a hot dog.

After describing Tillman, I told my friends, "He'll never be here tomorrow night." And he wasn't. His brother Richard accepted the award. After hearing me rave about Tillman and then seeing the Tillman film presentation the next evening, my friend—who has written more than two dozen sports books—exclaimed, "I should do a book on this guy!"

"Too late, pal. I've already started an outline on one, but his story is so remarkable and so unique that people are going to have a difficult time believing it. Plus, I'm having problems lining up interviews because he abhors publicity."

I returned home to Cape Cod and did little on the Tillman project, because finishing touches had to be done on two other books involving fans of the Chicago Cubs and St. Louis Cardinals. The months flew by. One morning at breakfast with an important business client near The Mall of America in Minneapolis, a glance at an overhead TV brought the terrible news: "Pat Tillman killed in Afghanistan." That couldn't be. Pat Tillman was never going to die, certainly not before me. This could not have happened, but it did. My breakfast guest was shocked by my reaction. Just like at the ESPY Awards, I once again explained the Pat Tillman saga. She said, "You've got to do a book on him! What a role model!"

So, the Tillman outline was retrieved, work started again and constant dead ends encountered. While it was admirable, almost incredible that Pat Tillman eschewed publicity as a player and a soldier, it is mystifying why so many teammates and friends are so reticent to talk. If my best friend died, and if he had done so many unreal things that he would be a wonderful role model for millions of people, I would shout his praises from the highest steeple. Pat Tillman's legacy can positively influence more people than any other athlete or soldier I can remember. As strongly as I feel about the positive impact this book will have on young Americans, and those stories should be told, I must remember that I might feel differently if he were my son. No one, nothing, can prepare you for the death of your son, regardless of the circumstances.

F. Scott Fitzgerald was correct when he wrote, "Show me a hero, and I'll write you a tragedy." Being Irish and having gone to too many Irish wakes, I'm used to sharing wonderful stories that celebrate people's lives.

Growing up on a farm near the town of Lost Nation, Iowa, I had avidly read every Horatio Alger-style book of John R. Tunis. Remember *The Kid from Left Field*, Clair Bee's Chip Hilton series, all of the Frank Merriwell and The Ozark Ike comic strips? All preached the virtues of hard work, perseverance, obedience and sportsmanship where, sooner or later, one way or another, some forlorn underweight underdog would succeed beyond his wildest dreams in the sports arena.

But, Pat Tillman was real life. He was more natural than Roy Hobbs. He was a "Rudy" with talent, a John Daly without the excesses. He was manna from heaven to the NFL and every other beleaguered professional sports league. The Washington Redskins were sold to Dan Snyder for eight hundred million dollars, although several other teams may have had a higher street value. More and more players were widowers by choice. Wilt Chamberlain boasted of having slept with twenty thousand women—I'm not sure that I've even peed that many times. General managers are hoping bail money doesn't count against the salary cap. Ravens fans didn't know whether to root for the defense or the prosecution. And, O. J. was down to about six commandments.

Then, along comes Pat Tillman, just as if he had been cryogenically frozen for forty years—from a simpler time when Elvis was the King, Little Richard was the queen, and Bruce Springsteen wasn't yet in middle management; when no NFL game could start after four in the afternoon because NFL Commissioner Pete Rozelle wanted every kid to be able to see the game in its entirety before bedtime.

Among the biggest obstacles in putting this book together was the problem of repetition. Sometimes repetition is good. For instance, in a book I did on Mike Ditka, seven people described the run Ditka made in Pittsburgh the weekend of JFK's assassination as the greatest run they had ever seen. Yet only one of those made the book. The editor didn't understand that when the reader was through with the book, few would remember the importance or singularity of that catch and run; whereas, if all seven had remained intact, everyone would realize that that one play summarized Ditka's persona and his career.

So, too, the repetition with Pat Tillman, except many times greater. It was overwhelming. Almost eighty pages were deleted from this book because there were constant, similar and duplicate testimonials. Even so, many remained.

Since the age of ten, I've been a serious collector of sports books. During that time—for the sake of argument, let's call it thirty years—my favorite book style is the eavesdropping type where the subject talks in his own words. In his own words, without the "then he said" or "the air was so thick you could cut it with a butter knife" waste of verbiage which makes it hard to get to the meat of the matter. Books such as Lawrence Ritter's *Glory of Their Times*, Donald Honig's *Baseball When the Grass Was Real*, or any of my friend Pete Golenbock's books like *Go Gators* or *Amazin' (Mets)*. Thus I adopted that style when I started compiling oral histories of the Mike Ditkas and Harry Carays of the world. I'm a sports fan first and foremost, I don't even pretend to be an author. This book is designed solely for other sports fans. I really don't care what the publisher, editors or critics think. I'm only interested in the Pat Tillman fans having enjoyable reading and getting their money's worth. Sometimes a person being interviewed will drift off the subject, but if the feeling is that football fans would enjoy their digression, it stays in the book.

In an effort to get more material into this book, the editor decided to merge some of the paragraphs and omit some of the commas which will allow for the reader to receive an additional 20,000 words, the equivalent of 50 pages. More bang for your buck, more fodder for English teachers and fewer dead trees.

It's also interesting—as you will find in this book—how some people will view the same happening in completely different terms. Plus, with this format, you will usually find that the most interesting stories are from people you've never heard of before. There was a thought of omitting the attempts at humorous headlines—some of the headlines in this book prove that truly great comedy is not funny—and eliminating some of the factoids since much of this book was written after Pat's death, but all his friends questioned on this matter unanimously nixed that idea. Some suggested, however, we should add the word "Dude" before every headline.

One unpleasant side story: When I told a lady friend in Georgia that I was going to finish the Tillman book, she said, "Pat Tillman was an idiot." I was stunned and could not believe what she had said. I quickly and strongly pointed out to her that it was the hundreds of thousands of idiots like Pat Tillman who died for this country, hundreds of thousands more idiots like Pat Tillman who were wounded in service of America, and the millions of others who served in our military that allow us to be so unbelievably lucky to live in a country like the United States. Americans are so fortunate and so blessed, yet so many of us are so spoiled and so ungrateful. Thank God for all the Pat Tillmans of the world.

Pat Tillman was an unorthodox man in a society where orthodox behavior has stifled creativity, adventure and fun, a society where posturing and positioning one's image in order to maximize income has replaced honesty and bluntness...Pat Tillman was my reluctant hero—a once-in-a-lifetime person...a principled man in a world of rapidly dwindling principles...a difference-maker on an indifferent planet...a man the way men used to be in an America that is not the way it used to be...a loyal man to team and teammates and friends in an age where most people's loyalties are in the wallet...a man who fought the good fight on the gridiron before joining America's Team to fight the Taliban.

I will never forget Pat Tillman because heroes—like memories—never grow old.

Rich Wolfe

Contents

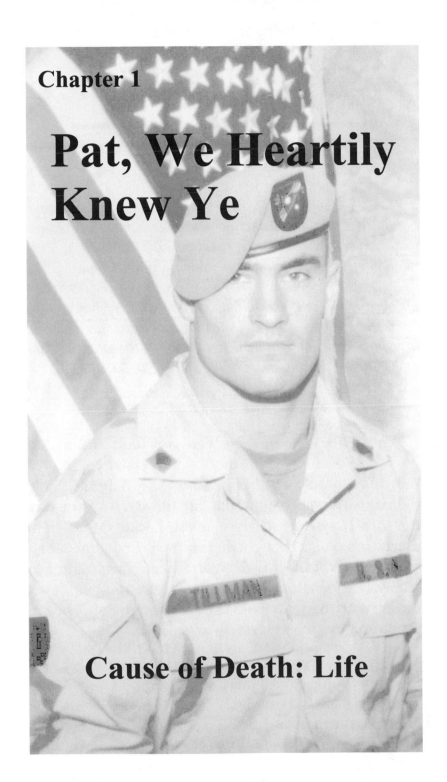

Chapter 1

Pat, We Heartily Knew Ye

Cause of Death: Life

IT'S HARD TO CHEER
WITH A BROKEN HEART

Jan Kalsu-McLauchlin

Jan Kalsu-McLauchlin, 56, lives in Oklahoma City, Oklahoma. Jan Kalsu is the widow of former star college and NFL football player, Bob Kalsu, who was killed on July 21, 1970 in Vietnam. He was killed by mortar fire on a jungle mountaintop base. Bob Kalsu was an All-American at the University of Oklahoma and was the Buffalo Bills' Rookie of the Year in 1968. Bob was the last NFL football player to lose his life while in action until Pat Tillman. Jan is proud to say that Bob's name lives on through his children, Bob, Jr., 33, and Jill, 35. Bob Kalsu had movie star good looks, great athletic ability, and grounded values. Bob Kalsu was a neat guy.

With Vietnam there were very high tensions. At the time, that America didn't have respect for its soldiers. My mind was on Bob the whole time he was over there…with Pat Tillman it's a tragedy that this has happened yet again. Because they both played football, it brought them into the limelight. It had to—look at what they'd given up to serve this country. In reality, I've seen this over and over again, and I've seen it mostly with the veterans I'd know through Bob. They're stand-up guys who represent all soldiers.

My son, Bob Jr., was the one who'd called me to give me the news about Pat Tillman. The question was, "Mom, have you heard the news?" I replied, "No!" My son informed me that Pat Tillman had been killed in combat, and my heart just sank. I guess, for me, because there

Jan Kalsu-McLauchlin (cneter) with Bob, Jr. and Jill

were close identities with Bob and Pat through football.… Aaah…my heart was torn open again. To have to remember again what I'd gone through with my family and to think about what Pat Tillman's widow and family were now facing—the same thing I struggled to deal with.

I'd gotten an e-mail from one of Pat's relatives, which made it easier now to reach out to the family but it was hard. I'd had a dream that Bob had been killed all over again the night after I'd received the e-mail. I was so glad when I woke up. I'm very aware of the extreme pain and stages of grief that they now have to embark on. There is nobody that can shield them from that pain—no words, no comfort can help with the stages of grief they'll have to go through to be able to face life again. You'll find yourself each morning asking the question, "How can I continue to live?" I was fortunate that I had two babies. I was told of my husband's death in the hospital room after having given birth to my son at midnight. I came home with a new baby and a twenty-month old daughter to take care of all by myself waiting for my husband's body to be brought back. It was the children, for me, that gave me the strength to go on each day and wanting to pass on the values of their daddy.

My heart goes out to the Tillman family. Believe me, it's hard because Pat leaves no legacy of children for them to see, reminding them of who he was through their eyes. At the time of Bob's death I kept thinking the man I loved is now gone forever. I didn't think about football, or anything else, just that he was my husband. The outside world saw Bob as a football player, but for me he was my husband and the father of my kids. He's gone and how can I make my children understand the same values that we had tried to uphold as a couple. You know, to be honest, as time went on during the Vietnam Era, it was very, very quiet, allowing me time with my kids. I remember seeing the mannerisms of their father acted out by the kids and you'd think that if Bob were alive, they'd have learned it from him. But to see this in them was such a wonderful feeling for me. It was like Bob was living through his children, and it brought me back to Bob, and I liked that feeling. I'm very spiritual in my faith, being a Catholic, and I felt as if Bob had always been with me helping to raise our children. The legacy of our love has lived on through our children, and now I can see it in our grandchildren. That love will be passed on through their children, too. I've always told my children how proud they should be of who their father was and to hold the name Kalsu very high and proud to honor who he was.

I feel for Marie Tillman…it's like your heart has been dropped on the ground and it's in a thousand pieces, and each day that you live, you try to pick up the pieces, crying the whole time. I don't know if Pat is buried near her home or his parents'. I remember, even with the new baby at the time, leaving them at home, when I went to visit Bob's grave. It's hard because of the fresh dirt on top and I wanted to lie on top of his grave and just cry, cry, cry! Being so close to him again made it so hard. In time, Pat's wife will feel this. She will also realize that Pat is with her, by her side. My heart goes out to her because she doesn't have any children. I don't know if this helps or hurts the healing process. I know that for me it helped me keep going and on the other hand it kept me from dating and going on with my own life. I didn't want to. I couldn't let go of my love for Bob. It was hard!

I didn't commit to my current husband for eighteen years after we had first met because of that love I'd had for Bob. I know Marie Tillman will hear lots of words of sympathy from people meaning well, but sometimes people say things that will simply crush her. Things said like "You're still young. At least, you can still get on with your life." Or, "You don't have any children holding you back." These things happened to me, and they hurt. I was polite, but I wanted to ask, "How can you say such a thing? I lost the love of my life." I think people at the moment sometimes just don't know what to say and they may reach for something. The best thing to say simply is, "I'm sorry," and, "You're in my prayers."

I can tell you right now that Bob Kalsu and Pat Tillman are standing together with their fellow soldiers who have died with them

I can tell you right now that Bob Kalsu and Pat Tillman are standing together with their fellow soldiers who have died with them. They're standing proud, representing America and what's right. The two of them would want to express to the American people to have respect for our soldiers, no matter what your feelings are towards them politically. The price of putting your life on the line for very little pay is a price not everyone is willing to pay for our freedom, and we shouldn't forget that.

I remember Bob was in the R.O.T.C. program at the University of Oklahoma. Part of that was signing a commitment stating you'll serve two years of active duty, and that's how he ended up in Vietnam. When Bob knew that, he had to tell the Bills, which was hard for him but they were very good with the news. Bob's daughter, Jill, was the pride of his life, and the day he got his orders for Vietnam, we both cried together because he didn't want to leave. He knew what a risk it was and Jill was just turning one year old. It didn't matter, because Bob made a commitment, and he was going to stick to it—that's who he was. He knew if he forced the issue, the NFL could have pulled some strings and got him out, but Bob was not that way. The hardest thing for Bob was saying goodbye at the airport the day he left. I recall that being the most memorable kiss we've ever had. As a Catholic, before Bob left, I went up and knelt at the tabernacle where the presence of God feels strongest for me. I said this prayer, "Lord, if you feel like you need Bob more that I do, at least give us a son to carry on his name." I remember also a time when Bob had the door locked to his room right before he was to leave for Vietnam, and he was holding our daughter, listening to her favorite record—just crying. It got to me. Then, right after he had left, I found out that I was pregnant. Bob never got to see his son, but he bears his name because I felt it was right. I'd visited Bob in Hawaii seven months into my pregnancy with Bob, Jr. so he could see Jill, and I remember what he said to me because it was our last words together. I told him, "Be careful" and his last words to me were, "No, Jan, you be careful because you're giving birth to our baby." He never knew it was a boy, not in that life but he knows now.

My greatest compliment to Bob's character wasn't that he was a great athlete or all of the other honors he'd had. I heard it when I talked to the other men that had served under him on Ripcord. On the day he died, they'd taken in over six hundred rounds of artillery fire on that hill. It's a wonder anyone is still alive. What I heard from those men is what epitomized who my husband was— Bob Kalsu, the officer and lieutenant. It was hard for an officer to have the respect of his men because they don't do the grunt work, they just gave orders. The men of Ripcord had such love for their officer Kalsu. That's why they were all there at Fort Campbell, Kentucky to honor him when the 101st Airborne named facilities there after him in memory of who he was. The men cried with me, because he took the time to get to know each and every one of his men, and he fought up front with his men in the trenches instead of staying back as an officer could do. Bob Kalsu wasn't a football player. He was a man, a leader, a man who cared, a real hero—Pat Tillman shared these traits.

Jan and Bob Kalsu

The last major leaguer to lose playing time during a season due to military service was Nolan Ryan of the New York Mets.

SEND A VOLLEY CHEER ON HIGH

Rocky Bleier

In many ways, Pat Tillman reminds people of Rocky Bleier, who served the country during Vietnam. Bleier wasn't given much of a shot to play in the NFL, despite playing on a national champion-ship team as a running back at Notre Dame. Bleier wasn't the biggest or the fastest, but he had determination, through which he made the Pittsburgh Steelers' squad. But after his first season, he was drafted for military service. He faced the challenge head on. Bleier suffered serious wounds in Vietnam. Through his determination and God-given ability, though, Bleier worked and became a valuable member of four Super Bowl teams for the Steelers during the 1970s. Today, Bleier lives in the Pittsburgh area where he spends much of his time as a motivational speaker. In nearly every sense, much like Pat Tillman, Rocky Bleier is a hero. Bleier's best selling book Fighting Back *became a well-received "made-for-TV" movie.*

My immediate reaction when I heard that Pat Tillman had been killed was simply feeling very bad about Pat and the whole situation. I was traveling on that Friday, and when I called back to my office, I was informed that Pat had died sometime Thursday.

I didn't know Pat but I knew of his decision to go into the Armed Forces with his brother. When he joined, I was asked a lot of questions about why he'd do it. I don't know because I didn't know him. But there really wasn't a comparison between Pat Tillman and myself, because

Pat made a conscious choice to do what he did for whatever reasons he felt were important, and I was drafted for Vietnam. The question here was whether Pat was true to himself and what he wanted to do in his life, which is admirable in today's society because we're faced with so much of a 'me' society. Maybe it's always been that way. Isn't it quite ironic that Pat's death came on the eve of the National Football League's draft? These young athletes are looking ahead to their careers, wondering where they're going to end up, how much they're going to make, and so on. Here was stark reality about Pat, a guy who was part of the football world but an example of other young people who have chosen to serve their country. The juxtaposition of the draft and Pat Tillman with hundreds of thousands of men and women who are serving their country was interesting to me.

Unlike Pat choosing to enlist, I didn't make a choice for Vietnam; I was drafted. Sure, I could've left the country and been arrested, or enlisted, or I could be drafted and put my two years in. During Vietnam, there were only a handful of players who had been in the NFL for a year and then fell through the cracks and got drafted for the war. Historically, if you made an **NFL** team, they put you in the reserves. That's what I thought. There was one guy, Bob Kalsu, who made a choice to serve. He was a starter, Rookie of the Year for the Bills, so he had a promising career. He was married with a baby on the way, and he chose to fulfill his commitment. It was a tough choice to make. Bob made it much like Pat Tillman made it, maybe for different reasons, but both had the courage to do it.

> NFL footballs are made in Ada, Ohio. Each team uses 1,000 per year.

I've read where people have wondered what made Pat Tillman different from anyone else. Given the circumstances, even those people in the reserves, when faced with a $3.6 million contract, who would give that up to serve when the stakes are so high? That's what made Pat Tillman different.

The guys with whom I served might have heard of me as a football player, although not to the same extent as the men and women around Pat. Of course, if the men with whom I served heard of me, they would had to have been avid Notre Dame fans because they wouldn't have known of me through the Steelers. Eventually, word spread that I had played at Notre Dame and one year in the pros, but it certainly didn't give me any breaks, particularly during basic training. I don't think that whole experience would've been any different if I hadn't played.

When we went to Vietnam, I got put in a line unit just like everyone else. Even when I joined the company, the captain said, 'Who's this smiling, strapping kid?' Funny, because there was only about two years difference in age between us, but a world of experience difference. He had been at the front line for awhile. I was the first 'new meat' they had in four months. New guys aren't readily embraced. You go in at the bottom of the totem pole. The guys in my unit were just guys. It didn't matter what you did before going to Vietnam. Your focus in that situation is staying alive, doing your job and working with your team—the platoon you were serving with. We didn't get personal. We knew each other by one name and we might have learned about someone's family, but otherwise we just survived, or at least tried to survive. One of the things that a draft Army misses is a sense of identity. Even today, as we've seen, units go over to the

Middle East as a unit and they come back as a unit. There's a sense of culture, camaraderie, team, we've trained together. That becomes very important. We didn't really have that during Vietnam.

People say I'm a hero for serving during Vietnam. It's humbling to hear that, but all I can do is shrug it off. Regardless, before the word hero is thrown around, you must decide how to define hero. All of us, particularly those people in the media, use the word so easily. The best definition I've found as hero came out of 9/11. The definition I heard was that a hero is someone who does what has to be done, when it needs to be done, without thinking about the circumstances. If you look back in history and talk to people who were labeled heroes, they say they didn't do anything special. They say they just did their job, or what was expected or what was needed. You react to a situation. Somebody's hurt, you just go in and get them, without worrying, 'What if I get shot?' If you're running through a burning building, you're not thinking about it. Much like the people who were killed on 9/11, especially in the towers, who were directing traffic and helping others, they simply reacted. They didn't worry. They were heroes.

It's nice when people say I'm a hero but the reason people perceive me in whatever regard is because I played football in four Super Bowls. So the story becomes I didn't give up, I persevered, good things happened. I could've played 11 years and not played for the Steelers in the Super Bowl. Would I have had the same impact in that case? Would the 'little train that could' story be the same with me? I often tell people that my greatest football game was when I was 9 years old and my career went downhill ever since. I played a game when I scored 51 touchdowns when I was 9. In high school, we went undefeated, I made all-conference, and Parade's All-American team. In college, I went to Notre Dame, didn't win any awards although we did win a national championship and I was a captain. I went to the pros and suddenly I had to struggle to make the team. Sure, we won four Super Bowls but I didn't carry the ball much anymore. It all went downhill since that game when I was 9 years old. So, if I hadn't played for the Steelers, would my story have had the same impact?

Pat, though, is very much a hero. He was doing what needed to be done without thinking about the circumstances. Not to be blown out of proportion yet not to be singled out, Pat's past profession raised his level of awareness in what was going on in the Middle East. If we're always looking for reasons of why things happen, maybe, just maybe, Pat Tillman can be viewed as a shining example or bring attention to the fact that everyday people are over there doing their jobs. They're fulfilling their responsibilities and we shouldn't forget them.

Another definition of hero can center on courage. There's a difference between courage and being a hero. Here's the example: you're walking past a river and someone seems to be drowning, or in trouble, and you can't swim. Do you jump in to save them? Usually not. That's not very smart because you both might drown. However, you jump in but you can't swim, but here comes a log. You guys grab on and someone pulls you in. The media would view you as a hero. I don't really think that person's being heroic as much as lucky. If the guy who can't swim runs to get help, not panicking, and finds someone who can swim or help otherwise, that's courage. It was courageous to take that step to find help.

He's not viewed as a hero, but it was courageous. Sometimes heroism gets blown out of proportion.

In Pat's case specifically, his story will be an inspiration to this generation and those coming. As it's told or as the books are written, it will remind people that Pat did stand for something. He was courageous and he was a hero. He accomplished quite a bit in a short period in his life. We as mere mortals have that capability as well. In Pat's case, it was being true to himself and how he lived his life. All of us are faced with choices along the way. Are we being true to who we are and do we have the courage to make that choice?

In our society, we are made up of three types of people—how we see ourselves, how others see us and what we truly are. Hopefully they become one somewhere down the line. We've known a lot of people who put up great fronts but they aren't what we see. We perceive people to be different than they truly are. I've heard the analogy is 'Fiddler on the Roof,' which starts off talking about traditions. Unfortunately, we get caught up in our own traditions in our culture. Sometimes we can't change, and ultimately we don't have the courage to change. That idea of being able to choose your life or make your choices becomes more difficult. With Pat, I hope he'll be remembered as someone who was true to whom he was and the choices or reasons why he was that way.

Sometimes things just don't seem to work out for the best. Maybe there's a reason Pat died. Maybe Pat will influence somebody who needed to read Pat's story and make a change in his or her own life.

THE MOST UNDERRATED ANNOUNCER IN THE COUNTRY

Tom Dillon

Tom Dillon was the voice of the Arizona State Sun Devils on radio from 1979 to 1998. Dillon has been the Fox Sports Net television play-by-play voice for ASU since 1998. He also did Cardinals broadcasts for 11 years, both as a play-by-play announcer and color analyst. He currently hosts a news-talk radio show in Phoenix.

The first time I saw him I thought he was kind of weird. He was one of those surfer type guys you wondered if he could play football. It didn't take me long to figure out he was a pretty good player. Every time he was out there he made a play.

He was one of those guys that look you right in the eye, assertive, which is unusual for a young kid. He didn't seem to have a laid-back attitude about him. He didn't mind talking to you, and he didn't mind using a few four-letter words. I immediately liked him. You get so many of these guys who mumble, don't shake your hand, and look at the ground when they talk to you. Tillman was none of that. He showed up for practice one day at ASU, and he's got on these weird looking pair of pants. I asked him where the hell he got those pants. He said, "I made them." I said, "What?" He said, "I can sew, and I make pants and sell them to my friends to make some money." I said, "I want a pair." He said, "Okay." So every time I saw him, even when he was playing for the

Cardinals, I said, "Where are my my pants?" He never made them for me. They were a throwback to the psychedelic colors of the 60s. It was something you knew Tillman would wear—completely off the wall.

> **"If you look up the definition of football player in the dictionary, Pat Tillman's picture would be there."**

It was so much fun to go do his games, especially when he got to the NFL. He was outstanding in college but when he got to the NFL everybody said he wasn't going to make it. He was too slow and too small. But the guy went out there and threw his body at people. I've always said to people, "If you look up the definition of football player in the dictionary, Pat Tillman's picture would be there." How can a guy make 200 tackles in a season playing safety?

He made so many plays, and he did so many things on the football field. I remember him a couple of times running across the field and making a tackle when he never should have had a chance to make the play. It seemed like he was always coming up with a play that even if it didn't win the game, it was a momentum-turner.

We had a lot of conversations over the years. I went out on several appearances with him. We did one in the summer, a Cardinals season-ticket promotion where we went out to neighborhoods in a motor home that was all decked out with Cardinal stuff. We'd set up shop in a neighborhood on a Saturday morning, the temperature was about 150 degrees, and a player would show up once in while. But when we said to Pat, "Are you going to be there?" He said, "Yeah," and he held court with the kids. Families would come around. He was just wonderful.

Every once in a while he'd get a little off-color. That was just him, and it never did offend everybody.

One of the things I remember about him is that he'd always try to slip in a four-letter word when I was interviewing him on the radio. He'd say, "Dude, are you going to have to bleep that?" I said, "Geez, Pat, give me a break." He'd just laugh.

I was sitting in the studio ready to go on with a newscast when I looked at my computer and a bulletin comes on that says Tillman was killed. I'm ready to open the microphone and say something and I can't believe what I'm looking at. I said to myself, "You have to read this." So I read it, thinking, "I hope I'm wrong." It was one of those things where you sit there thinking I had to be the one who told the people who listened to the station this morning that Pat had been killed.

We all knew Pat had a high purpose in life. The NFL was just a hobby for him. I know the world isn't going to be the same without Pat.

My favorite Tillman story…One day, a bunch of us are at (ex-Cardinal center) Aaron Graham's house. We're having a barbecue, drinking beer and sitting by the pool. We start to wonder where Pat is, and at that very moment, his shoes hit the pavement. Then his shirt. Then his shorts. We look up and Pat's standing on the roof of a two-story house in his boxer shorts. Of course, he jumps into the pool, and we all look over at Marie, his wife. She gives us a look that says, "I have no control over him when he makes up his mind to do something."
—JOE NEDNEY, Former Arizona Cardinals kicker

IT'S IN THE CARDS

Bill Dully

Bill Dully, 40, is a graduate of the University of Connecticut, and for the last three years has been president of Donuss—the sports trading-card company. Shortly after Pat Tillman's death, he was facing a Hobson's choice.

W ow...the Pat Tillman story about the jersey that we'd found. We buy about 10,000 to 13,000 jerseys each and every year. These include those of former players and even the most recent or current players on a roster, like Pat Tillman. We start the production process, cut them up, and make trading cards out of them for everyone. It's a simple production process that allows us to put a piece of the jersey right into the card. I remember back in 2000, we'd done a deal with the Arizona Cardinals, where we had paid for some signage in their stadium. As part of that deal, we got some jerseys. Pat Tillman's jersey was one of the jerseys we'd received. It's hard to believe but somehow it never made it into production even though it was on the inventory list. We'd done Tillman cards, but never a Tillman jersey card. Over a three-year period of time, with the rate we turn cards and jerseys, this is absolutely unheard of.

> **I looked at him and said, "This can't be true.**

One recent Monday morning we were at work, and one of the product managers, Joe White, came up to me, and said, "We've got a Pat Tillman jersey still inside the memorabilia room." I looked at him and said, "This can't be true. He hasn't been in the league now for almost two years." Joe said, "The jersey hadn't been cut or used and is still in perfect condition." I told Joe to go get that jersey, and he did. It was right behind Sammy Sosa's Cubs jersey. So, we are now holding an authentic game-used Pat Tillman jersey, guaranteed to be the real deal because it came with the certificate of authenticity. The jersey had torn sleeves, Astroturf markings on the shoulder, tar marks and even blood stains. So you knew this guy played pretty hard. The jersey certificate stated he'd tackled twelve members of the Dallas Cowboys while wearing this jersey.

What are the chances of something like that lasting three years?

It was on a team patch on the front of the jersey by the team logo and Reebok tag.

It's amazing that, at any given time, there were up to four thousand jerseys in that room, and Tillman's should have been used during the 2000-2001 season, but it wasn't. That was the year he had set the franchise record for tackles, and that would have been enough for us to use the jersey for production. We do about 20 football trading card sets a year, and in each set we do about 80 guys. That's about 1,500 guys whose jerseys we work with—passing leaders, rushing, tackling, receiving, and so forth. I don't know why it didn't get used. It was supposed to have been put into production, so it's a little odd or weird. It is very rare that this had happened, because it just doesn't happen. What are the chances of something like that lasting three years?

I thought that there might have only been six or eight Pat Tillman game-used jerseys out there at any given time. I've since talked with Pat's agent, Frank Bauer, twice. At first he stated "Look, we really don't want to talk right now about this or any of your ideas because the family is still grieving." I told him, "I'm Bill Dully, the President of Donruss Trading Cards," and he said, "I know what you guys do!" I had to explain that I wasn't calling trying to get a jersey. I had one, a complete jersey, and I think the jersey is very rare. I wanted to keep it whole and give it back to the family.

> **"You know, I've had over five hundred phone calls this week, and you're the only one who called to offer something instead of wanting something."**

You could hear a pin drop. That was the most chilling moment for me. I realized right then that what I was holding onto was something special. People loved this guy because he was not your ordinary guy. Just look at the lives he touched. I then began to think about the family and the human element. That's when Pat's agent said to me, "You know, I've had over five hundred phone calls this week, and you're the only one who called to offer something instead of wanting something." I told him that I have the jersey, and when things slow down he can call me to make plans for this rare jersey.

So, Frank Bauer called me back four days later and, once again, thanked me for offering the jersey. He reiterated the fact that I was still the only person who had called not wanting something about Pat from his family. Pat's agent said that he spoke with the family, told them about the jersey, and they want it! I'm now thinking this may be the only fully intact game-used jersey of Pat Tillman left. We are sure nobody did a jersey card of Tillman because the jerseys are turned over about every six games on the field. The piece that I've got is so tattered with the fourteen-game-used elements on it between the tearing, rain, blood, grass and so forth. Most of the jerseys are pristine or in perfect shape when we get them, but Pat's jersey symbolized his style of play: all out, where you leave nothing on the field. I think that this jersey means so much to the Tillman family because it's a piece of Pat; the blood, torn sleeves; these things represented who their son was, a son who gave everything he had to whatever he did.

I remember when Frank was silent because he knows what we do. We cut up trading cards and jerseys. Pat Tillman wasn't an Emmitt Smith, where we had done a lot of his jersey cards because of the demand, but Frank knew the importance of game-used memorabilia. Look, anyone can get a replica or a knock off Pat Tillman jersey, like the guy on ESPN was wearing. But you just can't get a game-used Pat Tillman jersey, and Frank knew that. So, I believe it clicked inside right away because he understands the business. This jersey is special. The jersey, when we bought it, was valued at $1,200. When I'd done an interview with ESPN.com, they'd asked what I was going to do with the jersey, and I told them I was thinking about giving it back to the family. The next thing I knew, because it happened so fast, was Donruss was on CNBC, CNN, Good Morning America, the talk shows and the list goes on. I couldn't believe it! I had an offer from a guy claiming to be an Arizona State graduate who wanted to buy the jersey for $50,000. He stated he was a big Pat Tillman fan. I also know of a man in Arizona who does a lot with game-used items. He has a game-used Pat Tillman helmet and this guy is well respected throughout the business. So, the helmet is more than likely the real deal. The guy does a lot with both Babe Ruth and Mickey Mantle baseball items, but he had the helmet because he was an ASU graduate and liked Pat Tillman. I was told that he was offered $30,000 dollars for that helmet from another Pat Tillman fan.

The choice to return the jersey to the family was ultimately my call, but there were six people involved, Joe White, myself and members of our sales staff. It didn't take long to conclude that we knew what was the right thing to do. This was after debate on our products, on how much money the jersey would bring, on Pat Tillman and the family. We did the right thing!

The jersey represents heroism, patriotism and bravery. This isn't what we do at Donruss. We represent and define sports—that is what we do. Babe Ruth defined baseball; baseball defined Babe Ruth, and his life was dominated by the game of baseball. So, cutting up a Babe Ruth jersey and putting a part of it inside a card is something I have no problem doing because when you get that card you can translate that story. But, with Tillman his history will be written by the stories and by people greater than a trading card company. We could have gotten the market's edge and crushed our competitors on this one because of our find. But it was an easy choice. We couldn't keep the jersey. It belongs with the Tillman family. We have no plans for any tribute cards or anything like that because we feel that this is so far out of our scope. To do something like that would be pretty tacky.

I served in the Navy and did time in the Persian Gulf. I knew the risks of what I was getting into, but, as a soldier, you don't think about that. It's not a choice. The choice is simple. That's why you're there. It didn't hit home to me at first, but when I saw the jersey and realized the sacrifice this guy had made for his family and everything that he had given up. I was kind of struck at first. I think I was taking it personal but then I felt a bit of pride overcome me because I realized he volunteered his services and life for this country; as I had made that pledge many years ago myself. There was a word that the country lost many years ago and it came back with what happened on 9/11,

...and that word is honor.

and that word is honor. I believe we lost this in the '70s and '80s, but it's back now through Pat Tillman because we do honorable things, and to be honorable is a huge thing to live up to and he did. This guy turned down a big contract. He wasn't driven by money in a society that is capitalist at most times, driven by money and greed. It's sad that success in life is graded by this first and not by who we really are—and for Pat to walk away from all of that...wow! He paid the ultimate price, but he has helped pay the country. There is an immeasurable sense of pride and honor to know we have special men and women fighting for this country. We should all treat our Armed Forces men and women with honor and respect. Try walking up to them, shake there hand, or hands and say "thanks for everything that you do." This is the greatest sense of pride and honor for them in which the act of shaking one's hand is a small task when compared to the larger one they carry for each and every one of us and the great country.

OKAY, JOHNNY RIVERS, HERE'S MEMPHIS INFORMATION

John Gall

John Gall was a childhood friend of Pat and Kevin Tillman. Later, Gall and Kevin Tillman were teammates in the Cleveland Indians system. Traded since to the St. Louis Cardinals, Gall drilled three straight batting practice pitches onto the berm beyond the left-field fence at Auto Zone Park in Memphis (arguably the finest minor league park in the country), wiped the sweat from his brow, squinted into the beautiful late morning sun and reflected on the Tillman brothers.

Growing up, I played against Pat and Kevin in baseball and football—I was in the same grade as Kevin. They were just great guys, and we played some summer ball together. In our little small-knit community, you just get to know one another. People sometimes don't understand California in the way it is. It really is just a bunch of smaller towns and communities, and it really feels like that sometimes. Even though I was just fifteen-twenty minutes away from them growing up, I still felt like I knew both those guys.

Originally it was Kevin who had decided he would go and join the Army Rangers. Pat, when he heard his brother was going to do that, wasn't going to let Kevin do it alone. Both of them have the same type of fire. They were connected at the hip as far as players growing up in our area. I am probably mostly concerned about what Kevin is going through.

Everybody here in minor league baseball was talking about it. There's nobody who would understand the sacrifice better than a professional athlete, to give up your dream, and, in his case, to chase another dream. A majority of the guys would never do what he did, and I think that's what makes this story different from anyone else. I would even say that ninety-nine percent of professional athletes won't do what he did, he was the only one that did, of anyone. We all sit around here and admire him, but I don't think anyone wants to step up and do it.

In the past we've all heard about and talked about Ted Williams and the other great athletes who went and fought in World War II. I guess we never thought about it happening in these days. One reason, the money is so great now. You've got a different class structure now with the modern-day athlete. That really changes things with the lucrative contracts and the fact that Pat was not a third-team, back-up guy. He was the real deal when it came to an NFL player, so obviously he had to sacrifice a lot more—not to say that certain World War II veterans who sacrificed their lives would have been worth any less, but, they definitely weren't giving up the riches that are there today.

The way Pat and Kevin were raised was just to live life to the fullest—at all costs. Obviously they were given morals and took them as seriously as anyone would when they were growing up. They lived by one way, and that was the right one, in their minds. They were never compromised.

THEY MADE IT TO CLOUD EIGHT

Paul Gero

Paul Gero has been a professional photographer since 1983. He spent nearly 20 years with newspapers, including the Chicago Tribune and the Arizona Republic. One of Gero's photographs has become etched in the minds of nearly anyone who has seen photos of Pat Tillman. In his first free-lance assignment for Sports Illustrated, *Gero photographed Tillman at the top of the light tower at Sun Devil Stadium. It was a place where Tillman often went to escape and think. In all likelihood, Gero probably was one of the few people who went with Tillman to that place of quiet solitude. Gero has his own studio in California, where he moved in 2002. He is a native of Columbus, Wisconsin.*

I don't think I'll ever forget the day I heard Pat Tillman had been killed. I was at the gym on the elliptical trainer when the announcement came on Fox News Channel. I was stopped dead in my tracks. There were about 25 minutes left in my workout, but there was no way I could continue. I was stunned. Immediately, I started thinking about how I needed to get home and look for a photo I had taken of him. I had a feeling others might be calling about it.

What photo? One in particular that I took of Pat at the top of Sun Devil Stadium in 1997 for *Sports Illustrated*.

That was my first assignment for SI For somebody who grew up on *Sports Illustrated*, it was a joy to work for them. I didn't know Pat, but I had heard stories about him. I thought photographing him was a great start for me with the magazine. They knew he was a scholar-athlete so they wanted shots in the classroom, in addition to action shots. I had some ideas for the portrait shot, but they were pretty ordinary. I first proposed the ideas to Pat while we were talking on the cell phone after he had spent the day with the reporter. He politely said something along the lines, "Mr. Gero, I don't mean to be difficult or a prima donna or anything, but that doesn't sound like me. Would you mind if we did something else?" I didn't want to make him uncomfortable so I told him we could. I asked his idea.

> **He thought for a minute and then told me how he sometimes climbed up the light tower at Sun Devil Stadium to meditate.**

He thought for a minute and then told me how he sometimes climbed up the light tower at Sun Devil Stadium to meditate. As soon as he said that, my jaw dropped. It was a photographer's dream. I never would have thought about that. I didn't even know he went up there.

The next morning, my assistant and I set up everything. We had a classroom set aside to show him in that setting. He was a real trooper. We spent about an hour on those. They were nice portraits of Pat, but they weren't anything spectacular. Then we went out to the light tower. It was impractical to take the big portrait camera up there, so I took the 35mm with me.

The climb up to the platform was only about 15 to 20 feet. The photo is a little deceptive because it looks like we're 400 feet in the air. We climbed up those little spikes like most people have seen on utility poles. Pat was wearing flip-flops and blue jeans, but he climbed it in no time. He then reached down and helped me out with all the equipment.

That was a natural place for him. He just took a spot. There wasn't any direction on my part. It was like being allowed in a kids' tree fort, in a way. That was his space. The light tower gave him a place to get away. When we went up there, he was like Rodin's 'The Thinker.' He was quiet and thoughtful. Pat was a deep guy. He was a strange blend of self-confidence without arrogance. He was comfortable in his skin.

That photo was taken in November, but it was still fairly warm. The conditions were a hazy bright. The view from up there, however, was incredible. It was spectacular with the mountains and the valley. You also could see airplanes on their approach, as they flew right over our heads. I can see why Pat liked that spot so much.

From a technical standpoint, it was a relatively easy shot. It's usually getting to that point where the photo happens. It's all about access. That's where Pat came in.

When I was up there, I could tell I was in the presence of a photo, but I didn't want to jinx it. So, I didn't tell anyone about it after I shot it. In my mind, I'm thinking double-truck, which means the photo covers two pages. But I couldn't really believe that, considering it was my first assignment for the world's best sports magazine. Shortly after I sent the film, the magazine's photo editor called me, ecstatic about it. And, sure enough, double-truck!

This might be the most famous photo I've ever taken, but that's all relative. The way the photo sums up Pat, I think it might be iconic…I think it's a true representation of him. I hope that in the future I have more photos of that caliber, and I think that's the way Pat would feel about things in his life. We should always strive to get better at whatever we do.

I didn't know Pat well. We didn't become great friends from that photo shoot. I covered the Arizona Cardinals for a couple years after he was drafted. He was always pleasant when we saw each other, but we didn't talk much. And, I always kept an eye on him to see how he was doing, even after I stopped covering the team. I always was amazed at his intensity, even during his first training camp. I remember noting, in my layman's way, how incredible he played during that camp.

All through my career, through photography, I've been taught to take photos of people where they're most comfortable. Pat was trying to be real with that spot. He wanted something that represented him. I don't know if he realized how incredible that was. I've always believed that people, subjects, give me photos. Pat certainly did that day.

When I heard that he joined the army, I wasn't surprised. It sounded like him. Obviously, we all hoped that it wouldn't turn out like this, but joining was him. He was something else. He's a hero.

We'd lay there, and Pat would always say, "There's more to life than football. I want to contribute to society and help people." I'd tell him he was going to be president, and he'd laugh. But I believed it.

—**PAUL REYNOLDS**, former ASU teammate

EQUAL RITES

Erin Foster

Erin Foster first met Pat Tillman at a surprise birthday party for Jake Plummer, while Tillman and Plummer were at Arizona State. She was struck immediately by Tillman's laid-back demeanor, and not being afraid to be different from the crowd. Erin and Pat developed a friendship that lasted throughout her moves to Hawaii and Washington. Currently, Erin lives in Washington where she works for Costco.

Before this happened to Pat, I'd think about him often, and about how he was an incredible person. He had so much energy and charisma. I have four children. One of my sons played football. I spoke with Pat quite a bit about getting some advice for my son because they had similar circumstances in their sports. Pat was willing to help out even though he had never met my son. It was wonderful that he would share with a complete stranger. Of course, you couldn't talk with Pat without the conversation going to other subjects, because he was a deep thinker. I've actually used Pat a lot in raising my children. I hope they are better people because of the advice and the way Pat lived. I really wanted to share that with my kids and hope they develop the same type of mentality and kindness. Pat was extremely special.

Really, I hope that everyone can see life through Pat's eyes, and the clarity in which he saw things. Life meant so much more to him than material goods. That's one of the very first things that struck me about Pat the first time I met him, which was at a surprise birthday party for Jake Plummer. They were still in college at the time. It was a big, stuffy party, catered, at some fancy country club in Phoenix. Of course, everybody wanted to impress. So, they came wearing their best jewelry and dresses, and the guys had the prettiest girl holding onto their arms. It was almost like a competition of sorts to see who looked the snazziest. C'mon, it was a birthday party! There weren't cameras there, there weren't scouts there, and there certainly wasn't anyone from the fashion industry there. Pat strolled in, wearing his totally casual clothes, the way most people would dress for a birthday party. It's hard for Pat not to stand out at that point. Regardless, he would have been the life of the party. Everybody wanted to talk to him. Everybody wanted to make time for him and he always made time for everyone. The fact that he had so much confidence in himself and so little care for the material things, made him stick out like a sore thumb, in a good way.

No matter what Pat wore, he was always the focus of attention. People were drawn to him. If people could see that they didn't have to be concerned with those types of things and still have the type of draw that he had, the world would be such a better place. If people had the sense of honor and pride that he had, not only for country—which is major—but also for family and friends. You hear his friends talk about him always being there for them and how they wanted to be better people because of him. They didn't want to disappoint Pat. That's huge. That's what I want to instill in my kids, that their words and actions can affect so many people. You have to remember that in the way you deal with other people. Obviously you want to treat others the way you want to be treated, but with Pat, it's a much bigger scale than that. He did it out of love and respect for the world.

People listened to Pat, even before he became a number on a jersey. Before Pat was number 42 at ASU and number 40 with the Cardinals, he could be identified in so many different ways. You hear the coaches talking about how Pat would show up at the football offices at an ungodly hour because he knew they would be there and they could talk about anything and everything. That's the kind of guy Pat was. You would hope that more people could be like that. He was a character.

The thing that I was most aware of with Pat during the time that I knew him was his relationship with men. He was probably one of the first persons I knew who was a big football player without any qualms whatsoever of embracing another man. Most guys won't be caught dead giving another man a hug, and showing that type of genuine affection. But, that's the type of person that Pat was. It didn't matter to him that he was seen hugging another guy and it might land on the front of a tabloid somewhere that "Pat Tillman is gay!" He wasn't concerned about that type of thing. He genuinely cared about people.

The relationship that he had with Jake Plummer is interesting to me. Many people feel that Jake brought Pat along with him. But, I don't know if that's necessarily true. Pat was the type of person who put himself in the shadows and allowed the attention to go to everyone else. He wasn't an interview kind of guy or someone who wanted to be the superstar on the cover of newspapers. He knew his job, he did his job, and he wanted to be a part of the team without being considered a superstar. That's so obvious by the fact that someone could walk away from the amount of money that he was capable of making to enter the Army.

Since his death, I find myself thinking about him on a daily basis, instead of occasionally wondering how he's doing. I followed his athletic career, and that continued after he went into the military. Where I live in Washington state, I drive past Fort Lewis on a weekly basis because my two youngest boys live down in Olympia. So, I get a huge sense of pride and an emotional rush when I drive past the base because I know that's where Pat trained for his military career.

I have collected almost every piece of literature that's been written on Pat since his death and I share it with my kids. Now all I can do is talk about him to as many people as possible and use him as an inspiration to the masses on how the world should really be. Heck, we wouldn't be going through all of this in the world if more people were like Pat.

I ran a marathon in 2000, and I was unaware that Pat had done one. Recently I had slacked off on my training, among other things. Because of Pat, though, I am now on my way to doing another marathon soon. I've jumped back in with both feet, wondering what in the world have I been doing? Oh, woe is me, life's so hard. When I feel like I can't take it anymore, I stick in the movie "Platoon" and that knocks me right out of my problem. I realize that I don't have it so bad. I've never fought in a war, I've never even heard—other than my shooting in a shooting range—a gun go off, I've never heard a helicopter crash. C'mon, I've got it pretty damn good. So, I'm out there now, trying to do some good because of Pat. I think many people who knew him have the mentality that "I don't want him to be disappointed by me." His energy will always be around us and I don't ever want that to change.

HE WASN'T A CARDINAL...
HE WAS A LION

Keith Currie

Keith Currie, who lives in Spokane, Washington, has the best of both worlds—an exciting career and a worthwhile hobby. For the past 17 years, Currie has been a program director with People to People. He's done sports photography since the mid-1970s. That hobby is how he met Pat Tillman, working for the Shriners during the East-West Shrine Game on January 10, 1998.

In 1998, I flew to San Francisco, and spent a week at the East-West Shrine game. That very first day is when I met Pat Tillman and the other athletes. Since I was a Washington State fan, I gravitated toward the Pac-10 players. Since I was there to photograph it for the Shriners, I met all the coaches and players, and went everywhere they went. We stayed in San Jose and practiced in Palo Alto. The game was played at Stanford Stadium.

During the week there were some great photo ops. The thing that really struck me, however, was going up to Sacramento to the Shriner's Hospital, which doesn't turn anyone away regardless of insurance or situation. One morning, we jumped on two buses and went up there, where we were greeted by then-Governor Gray Davis. We all went to the hospital after a nice lunch and the athletes walked around the different wings of the hospital and met the children. We went to a play area where the kids met these huge, strapping, All-American football players. It was fascinating to see that.

On the bus ride, I sat close to the front where the coaches were sitting. The players were in the back, meeting and enjoying each other. There was number 42, Pat Tillman. A lot of the guys had head phones on, listening to music or meeting each other. Pat was reading a book that had to be four inches thick. I didn't see the title, but Pat was the only one I remember with a book with him constantly. He carried it in the pocket of his baggy shorts, which he always wore. He wore flip-flops everywhere— he always looked like he was headed to a coffee shop or the beach. He wasn't big, but he was a lion. He was a unique individual.

Pat didn't joke around a lot or commiserate with the other guys too much. He was focused during the week of the East-West game. That was Pat Tillman, the Pat Tillman we've been reading about ever since he joined the Army Rangers, the Pat Tillman who starred for the Cardinals, and probably the same Pat Tillman from high school. He was focused and walked to his own beat.

When we got to the hospital, the mood kind of changed from goofing around or enjoying one another to more somber. The players knew they were there for another reason other than being seen by scouts in front of a national audience. They were there for the kids. I remember specifically watching Pat and seeing him play Foosball with the kids. He was every bit as competitive playing Foosball against these little kids, but eventually he relented and they got to win the game. It was amazing because he lit up around the kids. He was sort of a quiet guy, not really into the goofing around attitude.

But he lit up in that hospital. Once he got around those kids, it was a different Pat Tillman. Plus, the kids were drawn to him. Maybe because he wasn't much bigger than they were, especially compared to the other players.

My career is about bringing people together and breaking down barriers, which is why President Eisenhower started our company. I've always been patriotic and believed in bringing people together. When I heard that Pat walked away from the NFL and that lifestyle, it didn't surprise me. Not at all. When he passed away, and the way he was killed, it didn't surprise me that he was out front. He wasn't a Cardinal; he was a Lion.

It breaks my heart but you also know that there are men and women in the military, and others in uniform around this country, who are serving others. I only made it through Cub Scouts. I signed up for the draft but it was toward the end of Vietnam, and I never got called to serve. Now, I'm in awe of all the people who serve our country. That's what Pat was doing in the Army. He was serving our country. I think he's a hero. There's no other way to phrase it.

Pat was the kind of guy that you have a thousand stories about. One time he walked in and told me he was going to run a marathon and a triathlon. He wanted to stay in shape during the off-season. He just mentioned it, and the next thing I knew he had completed them both and did well in them. When he put his heart into something, he always got it done.

—MAR TAY JENKINS, Cardinals teammate

THERE ARE NO REST AREAS ON THE HIGHWAY TO SUCCESS

J.R. Rosania

J.R. Rosania is a trainer and triathlete in Phoenix, Arizona. He first met Pat Tillman when Pat wanted to train for a Half Ironman Triathlon. J.R. also was one of the first people whom Pat told that he was enlisting in the Army. This season, J.R. will be competing in the best-known Ironman triathlon, in Hawaii. He'll be racing for Timex in Pat's honor.

I first met Pat when he came to me for help in getting ready to train for a Half Ironman triathlon. When we met, we had a great conversation. We then met several times to review his training and to continue with progressing his program.

Even though he was referred to me, I definitely knew who he was, having watched him play football in Arizona for eight years. It was a thrill for me to train him, and we respected each other highly.

One of my favorite stories of Pat comes out of our training together. One morning, I had Pat work out with a fitness class I train. It's full of housewives and mostly women. It's a very tough workout with lots of constant activity. Pat and the ladies had a blast. He loved how hard they worked out and he kept encouraging them throughout the session. That was Pat. It was never about him. He was so quietly humble, you almost forgot about who he was at times.

Training for the Blackwater Half Ironman in Maryland, Pat was relentless in his training. In fact, I had to teach him to back off at times and rest his body. He was extremely disciplined and an extremely hard worker.

Pat came to me about four months before he was to report to boot camp and told me that he was enrolling in the Army. He wanted me to help him get into shape for it. He had such an incredible determination—that he ultimately took with him to his death—that I wasn't surprised when told me the news. I respected Pat so very much that I took it in stride, although I was concerned for his well-being.

I was SO HONORED that he wanted my help. I knew Pat trusted me, but when I had to swear to not tell "A SOUL," that trust was displayed. He said I was the first non-family member to know that he enlisted. So, at his request, it remained completely confidential.

Over the next 14 weeks, I drilled Pat. I tried to break him by putting him through training exercises I have yet to do to another person. They were things I knew he could get through, but would take him to the limit. In true Pat fashion, he trained his heart out. Before he reported to duty he told me, "JR, when I return, I want you to train me for football again and then we'll train for and do the Hawaii Ironman." I'll always remember that.

We didn't communicate after he was deployed. I wanted to respect his privacy.

This year, thanks to Timex, I will be racing the Hawaii Ironman in Pat's name and will carry his game jersey across the finish line. I then will have his name registered as the finisher. This race was one of Pat's goals when he returned. Since he won't be able to compete in it, this is one of the ways I can honor him. I will be wearing a pin and black ribbon with Pat's name and number given to me by the Cardinals, as well as an arm band with his number that every NFL player will receive for this season.

When I think about Pat today, courage, commitment, selfless, friend, someone without ego, all are phrases that come to mind. Pat's death makes me want to think less about myself and more about others. Also, it's taught me to be strong in my beliefs and go after my desires.

I trust who Pat was will live forever. He died for our country. He didn't just say things, he acted on them. I hope we all can gain from Pat's will and desire to constantly strive to become a better person and to live out our convictions.

I always thought, "Man, this guy is going to come back, play football again, star in his own movie, write a book." I laughed about it then, but it's hard to think about now. I can't believe he's gone. He gave up his life for our country. It's incredible—the selflessness. I told my wife that Pat he makes me want to be a better man. He makes me want to be a better person.

—STEVE BUSH, former ASU and Cardinals teammate

THE CLEVELAND INDIANS:
THE LAST REFUGE OF SCOUNDRELS

Jason Smith

Jason Smith, 33, is a scout for the Cleveland Indians, working primarily in the California area. He has been scouting four years, and he signed Kevin Tillman, Pat's brother, to a contract with the Indians. Smith developed a love of baseball during his time in college at Long Beach State University. He has a 2-year-old child and a beautiful wife.

I remember Kevin Tillman. I scouted his talents, attitude and athletic abilities. I'd identified Kevin as a prospect when he was a pitcher in college. I had written up a good report on Kevin and put him on my follow-up list like I would for any good, young prospect. I could just tell that Kevin was a tough kid by the way he went about playing the game and doing things the right way. Kevin was very professional, a born leader, blue collar, you could tell he had respect for the game.

I found out just like everyone else did about his decision to join the Rangers through the media sources. It was just something Kevin felt that he wanted to do. I prayed for Pat, Marie, Kevin, Richard and the rest of the family once I'd heard the news. I'd written the family a letter prior to the news about Pat in which I told them that I'd been thinking about the family for sometime. I wanted to convey my feelings about what a great job they'd done raising these three young men…but I just never got around to sending that letter. The letter was still sitting on my desk the day Pat died. I finally did mail it.

It was hand written. To it, I added my condolences after the news of Pat's death.

The athletes of today are big-money players with big signing bonuses, big houses, large contracts and nice cars. What Pat and Kevin did was special because they walked away from all of that and joined the Rangers. The two brothers took a position and followed through with that regardless of their position in society. They were special...special guys. They just got it!

I tell every player that I sign no matter what happens to them in their life that "I will always be that scout who signed you and opened that door to professional baseball." I like to think that my role with this job and the organization is kind of glamorous, but I'll never forget that I'll always have a tie to each one of those men, and especially Kevin because of his character. Kevin was such a great kid. He was a responsible person. When I found out once again he had enlisted—because of his morals, it didn't surprise me. I think of the word heroes when mentioning their names. That's not too strong a word—Kevin and Pat were true modern-day heroes, warriors, gladiators or whatever you might view them as. Pat was and Kevin still is *special*.

I like to tell the Frankenstein story about Kevin, where Burlington was playing a double-header as part of a rain make-up. The Burlington Indians, who Kevin was playing for, in Burlington, N.C., had a day/night double-header. I remember it as Kevin just having one of those incredible days where everything clicked, and he had went four-for-five batting in the first game and had four hits in the next game. Kevin had a single, double, even a home run, and he legged out a triple. It was just like everything was going his way. Kevin had been playing in the field and running the bases now for some eighteen innings, and it was in his final at-bat during the game. I think they've got it on video somewhere. Anyway, he stepped into the box and looked at a strike, and he then started stretching and moving around like he wasn't comfortable or he was cramping. Kevin swung at the next pitch and missed, and he kind of hunched over and staggered trying to keep his balance. Kevin was again trying to stretch so he could continue in the batters box. Finally, Kevin connected on a pitch, and he hit it hard. The ball was crushed—a line drive. Everyone thought it was gone—you know, another home run on what was a special day for Kevin. That's not what happened. After Kevin hit the ball, he just stood there...not trying to show up the other team; it was because his body had just locked up. The ball had fell short of a home run and hit the wall, and I don't know how he made it to first base. It was like Frankenstein-dragging-a-foot kind of humped-over movement, slow toward first base as he moved down the line. Once he got to first base, he collapsed. The trainer had come out to check on Kevin; he was severely dehydrated and had to be carried off the field to an ambulance, because his body just gave out on him. The story here is that Kevin, just like his brother Pat, never quit. It's part of their character.

I'd heard another story from one of the Burlington Indians managers about the time that Pat had came to visit Kevin. The guy telling the story described Pat as a Hollywood movie star walking into the stadium. He had long flowing hair and a cut jaw line like a Greek god. When someone from out of town, like Pat, enters a small town like Burlington, it makes an impact. He was described as being larger then life while he was there. I was told that

Pat was so happy to see Kevin and pleased about how well he was doing that Pat asked to take the entire team out for dinner. As you can imagine, it was quite a sight. Pat even took the coaches and managers. I think it was pizza and beer. Pat footed the whole bill. He was just that kind of guy!

I remember Pat and Kevin Tillman from about ten or fifteen years ago. The Tillmans were great customers, and that's the way I knew them—as customers. I own one of the oldest stores in town with a lot of football gear and baseball, too. And that's why they came.

I've had more than a million people in my store so it's hard for me to remember everyone, but I knew the Tillman boys because of their athletic accomplishments. I don't remember either one of those boys ever giving me a hard time, especially Pat. They were just good kids and not smart asses like some kids could be from time to time—wise guys, the kind that are sloppy dressed. Pat was always dressed nice and was always polite I remember that about certain people

My customers have been talking about this a lot since San Jose was his hometown. There just aren't too many guys made like Pat Tillman. He was special, and you've got to be in order to do the things he did for his country. Pat was no Joe Blow…just look around. It takes a special type of person to do this. He gave up all that money to go half way around the world to fight in a foreign country.
—JERRY FONTANETTI, 70, owner of a sporting goods store in San Jose, CA

The Mark Cuban Foundation's primary function is to help people. One of our endeavors was starting the Fallen Patriot Fund. It was formed to give out grants to soldiers' families who lost loved ones in Operation Iraqi Freedom. Mark had taken it upon himself to match all donations to the fund, up to one million dollars. He also got the Bank of America involved with donating to the cause as well. Mark has a big heart, and I know this was just something that he felt he wanted to do. He always likes to share, and we know he has the financial means to do so. I have been very busy reviewing the applications that have been coming in looking for support. I wish we could say there haven't been a lot of them, but I can't...we wish this wasn't the case. We can't give money for education or travel purposes, only for immediate financial needs or transitions such as when the bread winner was killed or seriously injured in combat. The total number of families helped to this point is thirty-two out of well over two hundred applications that we've received.

I was sad for Pat Tillman and his family when I first had heard the news, just as I would be for any soldier who had lost his or her life in combat. I have no opinion on whether Pat Tillman was a hero or not—I'll let the media make those assumptions. The loss of life is tragic, whether it's Pat Tillman or any other soldier. Who's to say one outweighs the other.

The media attention is going to have an impact on our donations and that's good. If it can help these families who have lost so much, the bread winners who supported their family's way of life. It's at that point; we then feel we can help the families through the tough transition period.

—**Brian Cuban**, 43, Executive Director of the Mark Cuban Foundation and co-founder of the Fallen Patriot Fund. His brother, Mark, is the billionaire owner of the NBA Dallas Mavericks

Chapter 2

Arizona, Arizona, Arizona State

**Fight, Devils Down the Field
Fight with Your Might and
Don't Ever Yield**

WHEN ASU CALLS, YOU GOTTA ACCEPT THE CHARGES

Dick Arbuckle

Dick Arbuckle, 64, was the special teams coach at Arizona State University who recruited Tillman to ASU.

I got lucky recruiting him. I was able to see something a lot of other people didn't. When we brought Pat over here, and Bruce Snyder interviewed him, he saw something special also. We all benefited from that relationship.

The San Jose area was my recruiting area, so I was pretty familiar with what was there, but Pat was kind of a guy who was under the radar in terms of high visibility; he had low visibility. But I had an opportunity to watch him play one Friday afternoon when ASU was playing in the Bay Area. Of course, coaches would go out to recruit wherever we went, and so I stopped by to watch him play. I was just so impressed by his intensity, his enthusiasm and, of course, his performance. He was so far above all the other players on his team and on the opponents team as well. I came back and talked to Bruce about Pat Tillman and raved about him. Bruce said, "Who's recruiting him, who's recruiting him?" I said, "Well, uh, I don't know if anybody other than San Jose State is recruiting him." The other coaches were looking at me like I'm nuts. Finally Bruce sent secondary coach Donnie Henderson over to look at him, because we were wondering where he was going to play. Donnie came back and said, "Well, I like that kid also." So, Bruce gave me the okay to bring him in for a recruiting trip. Through the interview process, we were extremely impressed with the young man. If he wasn't the last recruit we signed that year, he was pretty darn close.

I started playing him on special teams as a freshman, and I think he played on every one of the special teams except maybe our field-goal team, and he could have probably gone in and kicked field goals if you'd ask him. He did a terrific job for us and as years went along he continued to play special teams. There were some games where he'd play ninety snaps—every snap on defense, then all the special teams' snaps. He was a pleasure, obviously, to coach.

> **I've coached some good players, but in terms of the whole package—personality and everything else— there's been no one like him.**

It was quite a process discovering how good he was. That freshman year as he performed on special teams, he was way beyond his years and maturity level. The defensive coaches started taking notice of that, and I think he just established himself at that point—that he was a guy who was going to play and be a big help to us. Obviously he did.

I've coached some good players, but in terms of the whole package—personality and everything else—there's been no one like him. He was a unique individual.

PAT TILLMAN WAS JUST A REGULAR GUY WHO SOMETIMES WORE A CAPE

Mark Brand

Mark Brand has been the assistant athletic director/sports information director at Arizona State for over 20 years. He was the SID when Tillman played at ASU. Mark has been directly involved with the football program for many years and knew Tillman well. He was very instrumental in the arrangement of all the posthumous ceremonies in the Valley.

This is one of the more amazing stories about Pat. During the 1996 season (11-0, Pac-10 champions and Rose Bowl participant), we went to UCLA with a 5-0 record. UCLA had invited ten to fifteen thousand school kids to attend the game free. When we came out of the tunnel, they were booing us—loud. They loved the Bruins!

We were down 28-7 at halftime, and they kept on booing us as we ran through the tunnel toward our locker room. Then in the second half we began making plays, and Pat was making many of them. We came back, and the kids began cheering for us. When we won 42-34, Pat sprinted down to the end zone where the kids were now screaming for us, and he led them in singing our fight song. That was a scene I will never forget.

When he was a freshman, he would sit in his position meeting listening to Lyle Setencich, linebackers coach, who would ask questions about, "If the offense does this, what would we do?" An answer would come, and Pat would yell out, "Wrong!" And if another player answered another question, he would state loudly, "Wrong again!"

During his sophomore year, the coaches took him out on third-down situations, and he wasn't happy. He would stand on the sidelines screaming, "TD this play!" He figured if he wasn't on the field, the other team would score. He would always stand next to Phil Snow, defensive coordinator, on the sideline just waiting to go back in.

All freshmen have to take a mandatory orientation class; it's a study hall class. One day Pat and Jeff Paulk were supposed to meet with an academic advisor, Mike McBride. Jeff showed, but Pat didn't. When Mike found him later

When Mike asked the coaches about Pat, they said "There's a kid you will never have to worry about."

and asked where he had been, Pat replied, "No offense, dude, but I don't need it. So there's no need to waste your time." When Mike asked the coaches about Pat, they said "There's a kid you will never have to worry about."

One time I had set up an interview for Pat with a reporter, but at the designated time, no Pat, and he always showed when he said he would. I finally found him upstairs in the ICA building where he was tutoring his teammates. He wasn't a tutor, but he was once again helping his teammates. That's the kind of person he was.

When another member of the athletic department had dinner with him in Seattle in January, Pat asked about every member of the department—not just some, but *every* one. He loved ASU and the people here that much.

Some seven years ago, Carter De Haven, the producer of the movie *Hoosiers*, among others, received a letter from a movie fan telling Carter how much he had enjoyed the movie. He said it was the best sports movie ever made, and thanked him for making a film depicting the success of such overachievers. That fan was Pat Tillman. Since Pat's death, Carter has indicated he would be interested in making a movie about Pat. Now that is irony.

Pat would climb one of the light poles at Sun Devil Stadium to just sit and look out over the Valley. He would read, study and meditate. We never knew then. We found out more than two years later he had done that.

He never sought publicity, but once he entered the U.S. Army he knew it was coming. I once told him his life had changed forever. He didn't want to admit it, but finally he did. He said, "I know. I know."

Everyone in this department who knew him learned so much more from him than he was ever taught here. He was the most unique person I have ever met.

> Keith Smart's shot to win the 1987 National Title came on the very same night that the movie "Hoosiers" narrowly missed winning an Oscar.

TILLMAN WAS VERY INTELLIGENT... BUT OTHER PLAYERS TRIED TO SIT NEXT TO A SMART LEFT-HANDED STUDENT

Mike McBride

Mike McBride, 43, has been manager for academic services at Arizona State since 1994.

I came in as a new academic advisor in September of 1994. I was assigned all the freshman and sophomore football players. Pat made quite an impression. What was interesting was when we started study hall, all the freshmen go through it together. I gave an introduction on study skills, what professors expected of you, why you wanted to connect. Pat was there but when study hall started he wasn't there that first day. I went to coach (Donnie) Henderson who was running study hall and asked where Pat was. He said he didn't know where Pat was but would check into it. The next day was the same deal; he wasn't there. I'm in my office a couple of days later and Pat comes rolling in. He said, "Hey Mike, I understand you've been looking for me. No offense, but I don't need this. I'm not going to embarrass my university." He was an unreal kid.

> "...I'm not going to embarrass my university."

The same meeting Pat kind of asked me—I think he knew the answer—"How many credit hours do you need to graduate?" I told him he needed 120, and he said, "It will be your job to make sure I don't get any more or any less." He had this presence, and he kind of led you. It didn't matter how old you were or if you were in charge. He wanted you to know he was in charge and had things together.

> **He probably was one of few people who read through the entire university catalogue.**

The interesting thing with Pat is if one of the other guys needed help, Pat would sit down with the guy and explain things. If I asked him to come in and do that, he showed up and would help the guy as much as needed.

He had very little use for anybody that would help him. He just had things under control. He probably was one of few people who read through the entire university catalogue. That's a contract a student has with the university, and when students have a problem, advisors ask, "Did you read the catalogue?" Well, it's 400-something pages, ungodly long, but Pat probably did read it. He knew all the answers.

Pat did everything in a real proud way. He was so special in the way he handled himself. He took great pride in that.

He won the NCAA post-graduate scholarship. Very few student athletes win that award. They give out a maximum of 175 a year.

I left for two years when Pat had gone into the NFL, because our family opened some businesses in the Valley. I talked to Pat and asked him if he would come to the grand opening. I said, "I'll pay you." He said, "Bull____,

I'll be there, you don't have to pay me." He came and signed autographs all day.

Going into his second year as a Cardinal, it had to be late June, early July, I'm walking through Barnes and Noble and there's Pat sitting at one of those bistro tables. He has these stack of books sitting there. I said, "What do you have here?" If I remember, he had history books, something from Hemingway, short stories. He said, "I'm getting my training camp reading list ready." You have images of everybody else hanging out in town, and there's Pat—under a tree reading Steinbeck or U.S. history or tales of World War II. He had a curiosity about everything.

Pat was just unusual in the way he carried himself and the way everybody followed him. He was confident but he wasn't cocky. He wasn't arrogant about it. He was one of the few guys I remember who could tell people what they needed to hear but didn't want to hear, and he could get away with it because they respected him.

"I was raised thinking everything is either this or that, black or white, right or wrong, but Pat could live with *and*. You could play football *and* be an intellectual. You could be courageous *and* sensitive. Because of Pat, I've become more and more of an *and* person."

"I almost naively had a sense that the guy was indestructible and invincible and was so smart and so athletic and so courageous that he would be fine. Obviously, war is a difficult thing, and those things don't hold up."

—**Bruce Snyder**, Former ASU Head Coach

TILLMAN'S #42 TO BE RETIRED. JACKIE ROBINSON HAS ELITE COMPANY NOW.

Connor Banks

Connor will be a senior linebacker/defensive end for the Sun Devils this fall, and will be the last man to wear No. 42 for ASU. He has had the number for his entire career, and the school decided to let him wear it one final time before the school retires the number along with three other names (and numbers) that are shown at Sun Devil Stadium. Connor hails from Richmond, Calif., a northern California community much like Tillman—another factor in the decision to let him wear the number this fall.

My life has changed a lot. I'm not used to doing interviews for one thing, and I wish they were for my football playing and not this. This whole experience has made me examine how I was living and make me want to live life the right way. I want to get to the point where I can say I'm striving to accomplish everything I can like Pat Tillman did. The guy gave one hundred percent in everything and without question was always striving to be the best. I will carry the U.S. flag every time we take the field this fall, both at home and away. All I can do is wear No. 42 and try to do my best all the time. I don't see it as a burden. I see it as a responsibility that was bestowed upon me. I embrace it. You can't really live up to somebody like that. It's an almost-unattainable goal. The best I can do is strive for it. It gives me a lot of pride to wear the number that such a great person had. It's going to motivate me even more to play to the best of my abilities, knowing he will be watching, that he'll be "there" for every down this year.

It's a great honor. I feel so much pride for what he has done for the community and this nation. For him to give up his football career and go overseas to fight for his country and fight for what he feels is right is a great thing for the nation. I want to send my prayers to his family.

It's crazy because some people just come up to me and say, "We're really proud of you." People, even in my class, say, "I appreciate what you're doing." It's so hard to wrap my mind around. No parent should lose a son.

No matter what your political beliefs are, having a person like that stand up for what he believes is right, being willing to go and fight and sacrifice his life makes you feel we can get everything going in the right direction.

When I was a freshman, under Snyder's staff, Coach Snow, who knew Pat really well, would tell us about different players he had coached, and he always mentioned Tillman. I've watched tapes of the Rose Bowl, and saw how he played the game. He played with so much passion. When you look at him, you say, "That's a football player. That's what I want to be."

I think it says being materialistic isn't the most important thing. It puts everything in perspective for us and shows what is important to people. Sports aren't everything. You need to do what you think is right for you and your family. Pat's death wants me to push even harder. I just have more ambition to try to fulfill everything I want to in my life. I want to achieve as much as I can.

LET US NOT REGRET THAT SUCH A MAN DIED, LET US REJOICE SUCH A MAN LIVED!

Sharon Meany

Sharon has worked in the ASU athletic department for years in various capacities, and has come across numerous athletes in her time. She always liked Pat, and like Joanne DeMassa, found him delicious to look at. Sharon has worked in the ticket office and as a secretary at ICA. Her husband, Paul, played basketball at ASU under recently deceased and longtime ASU coach Ned Wulk.

I saw Pat a few times a week when he first arrived at ASU. I worked in the ticket office when he came in as a freshman in 1994. The one story that comes to my mind is when I was talking to him about this big story on cloning sheep. I told him I don't believe in that stuff—I think it's against God's nature, God's will. But I told him, "In your case, gorgeous, I would make an exception." He looked at me like what was I talking about! He couldn't figure out that I thought he was really good-looking. That was when he still had the long hair, which I still think is when he looked the best.

We're collecting as much Pat memorabilia as we can send it to our son in **Missouri**, because we want our grandson to know about Pat Tillman. And hopefully he will try to emulate Pat. He'll be somebody I'll remember my whole life.

> In the 1983 Holiday Bowl, Brigham Young University quarterback Steve Young caught the winning touchdown pass in a 21-17 victory over Missouri.

Remember the George Patton quote, "Let us not regret that such a man died. Let us rejoice that such a man lived!"? That almost seems like it was written for Pat.

That reminds me of a man who came to ASU today. He had written a song about war and soldiers, and it was so good Reba McIntyre sang it when she appeared here at Country Thunder. The day they burned the CD with that song was the day Pat died. And now they're handing it out to anyone who wants it. He gave me one, and I can't wait to listen to it.

The first time we football secretaries saw him, we just swooned. I told Phil Snow, the defensive coordinator, that Pat could come up to the office any time. Phil just rolled his eyes. We've had lots of players come up to see the coaches, but there was just something about Pat. I couldn't put my finger on it, but there was something about him.

One time we had a female student come up to my desk and say sheepishly, "I feel so stupid but there's a football player in my class I'd like to know. Could you tell me his name?" I said, "What does he look like?" She said, "Well, he's really good looking. He has long hair...." I knew who she was talking about right away. She told me she simply had to stare at him during every class, and she was getting nothing done in the class, and she would have to drop the class if she couldn't get to know him. We all laughed.

I got to talk to Pat quite a bit when he'd come up to see Coach Snow and Coach Lyle Setencich. He was a great young man.

—JOANNE DEMASSA, retired lead secretary, ASU football

JONAH WAS RIGHT, IT'S HARD TO KEEP A GOOD MAN DOWN

Brent Rich

Brent Rich was the team physician at Arizona State University from 1993 to 2003.

The thing that was nice about Pat was that he was different from a lot of the athletes. He'd go out of his way to say hello. I remember times Dr. Debbie Garland and I would be at lunch, and he'd see us and say, "May I sit down and have lunch with you guys?" Other athletes wouldn't feel comfortable in the situation. We'd sit and talk but we wouldn't necessarily talk about football with Pat. You'd talk about how life was. He just seemed so much more advanced for his age. He seemed so much more mature. On the other hand, he was sort of a rebel. He did his own thing. If there was something crazy going on, Pat was probably in the middle of it.

I was trying to think if we saw him for any specific **injuries**; I don't ever remember him being hurt significantly or for any period of time. He was bruised all the time,

> Almost every good football team at any level in America is one play (injury) away from being average. Average time lost due to injury in high school football is six days. Healing time due to injury to a high school cheerleader is 29 days. Among the sixteen most popular college sports, spring football has the highest injury rate.

but he was one of those guys who just rubbed dirt on it and kept playing. If he was hurt, he didn't come to us, or he played hurt.

There is one story that says something about his character. One of the students was doing an article about the rituals athletes go through. This student wanted to meet Jake Plummer, Keith Poole and Pat. When Pat became aware of that, he was as thrilled to talk to this student as she was to talk to him. He was thrilled that she was interested in him.

He was fairly boisterous in the locker room before games. Some guys get quiet and introspective. He'd try to pump guys up and yell and scream. He dropped a few words, but he really tried to motivate and bring everybody up to his level of excitement. You know how some guys are a quiet leader. He was more of a boisterous leader.

He kind of followed Bruce Snyder's philosophy that nobody beats us in our house. Nobody wins at Sun Devil Stadium. That's our place.

One good memory for me was when we did go out and party. Many times he would just go home and talk to his girlfriend, Marie, now his wife. He'd be on the dance floor *by himself.* He would be dancing, long hair in his face, looking down at the dance floor. He was jamming. He'd walk around feeling good about himself. And we'd all laugh, because, with Pat, that was all you could do. Then he'd start laughing, too.

—SHAWN SWAYDA, ASU defensive teammate and friend

ASU:
TRUTH, KNOWLEDGE, A GREAT TAN

Doug Tammaro

Doug Tammaro is the assistant media relations director at Arizona State University, where he became a close friend of Tillman. They spoke often during Tillman's time in the service.

P at was just a good guy. He related well to NFL players, but to the common folk out there he was a favorite. He was one of "them".

I remember what Pat told me before he went into the service. I didn't know what he was going to do. He said it was time for a new challenge. There were no specific things. It was something he had mentioned before, something he had thought of before.

He left me a long voice mail on April 1. He said, "Hey, I'm just training, dude, getting ready, staying in shape. Thanks, dude, talk to you later." He was getting ready to go back. He was excited to be going back overseas.

> **He left me a long voice mail on April 1.**

I have a picture of Pat in my office, his hair flying. It's so Pat. You had to know him to appreciate what a great guy he was. A lot of people don't know that we wanted to do a picture of Pat in last year's football media guide with his Army uniform on and the American flag in the background. He called me and said, "Dude, if you want to put me in Sun Devil gear, that's fine, but leave the Army stuff out." He never wanted the attention or considered himself special. The first thing Pat would tell you is, "My brother, Kevin, is fighting, too." He'd also tell us thousands of others are over there. He was just one of many—but a special one.

I remember when he was in college, somebody asked him about his GPA, and he said, "It's 3.8, but you don't have to shout that from the rooftops." That was Pat. He was really honored by the award he got at the ESPYs, but he didn't have to have that stuff.

> **The first thing Pat would tell you is, "My brother, Kevin, is fighting, too."**

When Pat was a rookie in the NFL, we asked him to sign 250 copies of a book we had published about the history of Arizona State athletics. He came over one day and signed them all. A couple of days later we called him and said the books he signed had been lost at the printers. Mark Brand, ASU's associate athletic director for media relations, apologized and asked if Pat would sign another 250 if he brought them to his house. Pat said, "Dude, don't worry. I'll come over." Later that day he came by and signed 250 more.

We had dinner on January 30 at the Flying Fish in Seattle. I was going to drive to the base, forty-five minutes away, but Pat said, "We'll drive in to see you." I felt like I was the guest of one of the most popular people in America. During dinner he asked about everything inside the athletics building. He went through the 1996 football roster, and he asked if I talked to former teammates, Jason

Simmons and Grey Ruegamer. He said, "How's Pat Murphy, the baseball coach, doing?" Then he said, "We have to make sure Rob Evans, (the basketball coach), gets it done." Somebody asked him if he was going to play football again, and he said he hadn't really thought about that.

We talked about what he was doing, but I didn't get into details. He knew he was going back. I said, "Man, you look bigger." He said, "No, dude, I'm wearing a lot of shirts." He had seen combat but it wasn't something overwhelming to him. He was private about that. I walked out of there fascinated. I never felt so good about a dinner in my life."

The next time I hear an announcer talk about some athlete's "heroic" performance, I hope he follows it up with, "Just like Pat Tillman's." Maybe that will keep the use of the word in the proper context.

—KEN PFRANG, Mesa, Ariz.

Pat Tillman wasn't satisfied just taking up space. He had to do more. And that's why his name and his sacrifice will be remembered long after his football career would have ended.

He made a difference.

And how about the rest of us? What are we doing? Why is it that a few hundred thousand Americans risk their lives in what has become a dangerous and dirty war, while the rest of us complain about $1-a-gallon gasoline?

—STAFF EDITORIAL, *The Arizona Republic*

PAT TILLMAN WAS GOD'S WAY OF BEING NICE TO ASU

Mark Zimmer

Mark is the manager/equipment operations and product fulfill-ment for the ASU intercollegiate athletic program. As the main man when it comes to uniforms and equipment, he gets to know almost all of the Sun Devil athletes. His thoughts on Pat come from a man who sees all in the locker room, where the uniforms come off and the personalities turn on.

I was here at ASU for Pat's freshman year and then for his senior year. Pat was a very matter-of-fact guy—did the right thing, did what we asked him to. There was no nonsense about it and no crying about it. No questions like, "Why do I have to do it this way?" His locker was always neat and clean, which may sound funny, but we see that the people who keep clean, tidy lockers, unless they're just a far superior athlete, they get the job done. When he was out with his buddies and his teammates, I know they had their own fun. He would go out and drink beer with the guys.

A lot of people live in the "now" moment, but Pat lived in the "next" moment. That goes all the way back to when he talked to Bruce Snyder about red-shirting. I remember seeing him numerous times in the locker room, on campus, in the building with his backpack on heading wherever. He wasn't one to sit around and lounge in the locker room and hang out. There's always seemed to be a purpose for Pat Tillman.

I do remember that we never had a problem with Pat. From an equipment manager's standpoint, if you picked a hundred names out of a media guide, I'll guarantee you there are probably some guys who I'd say, "That guy's a jackass." But we never had a problem with Pat. A reporter called me last week and wanted to know if I had a favorite Pat Tillman story. I said, "Bob, it's going to be a real boring story for you because I don't have a favorite story; I can just tell you that he was never a problem." In some circles, he was so direct and to-the-point. He took care of his own business. He didn't even use an academic advisor; he took care of all that himself. He also tutored other people. He was very unassuming. Here's a guy who, by all accounts, could have been an absolute jerk—good looking guy, smart, intelligent, awesome athletic ability compared to the next guy. He didn't fall into the trap of a big ego. When he was a senior, it seems like he was always in the right place, at the right time, doing what he was supposed to do. He was a little more vocal than most, but he wasn't a rah-rah-rah type guy. He did his thing. He always had a pretty serious look on his face. He was always real polite and outgoing. He didn't smile very much. Whenever you talked with him, the minute he opened his mouth, he was always friendly.

About five of us had a meeting last night. I said, "You know, he didn't sit at the back of the bus. He and his other Afghan military guys who were killed weren't at the back of that vehicle. When they said they were chasing after somebody, he was out front. You know that for a fact. He wasn't waiting for someone to tell him where to go." It would be like, "Here's where we're going." That was him.

Even before all this happened, Pat Tillman was one of my favorite guys. It didn't take this. This wasn't a wake-up call to Mark Zimmer to the kind of guy Pat Tillman was. I remember telling my wife, when watching Cardinal games or just seeing him, "He's such a nice guy to be around. He was truly one of the good guys." I like when the "good guys" come back, when they stop in the building, it's always good to see them. Too often we get the schmoe, the jackass that comes by, "Hey, you got any T-shirts for me? You got any shoes for me?" Pat never asked for anything. We just had the spring game a few weeks ago, and I had four or five guys come up and say, "Hey, what have you got for an old ball player?" Yes, he was one of my favorite guys even before this all happened.

I don't think there will be a coach at any level who won't use him as an example of how to live your life. I don't think it's possible there will be a coach out there who won't, at one point or another, use him as an example of what's happening and the way you should try and do things. It goes beyond football coaching and playing football – it goes to style of life. I wouldn't care whether I was coaching football or working with the ministry. The kids will listen because he was a football player, but the message should be heard by all. I think that's very true. I don't think there's any question about that. He did things that you try to strive to get people to believe in and in the way we do things.

—DAN DUNN, head coach, Mesa Community College, Mesa, AZ

YOU CAN'T GET INTO HEAVEN UNLESS YOU'RE A SUN DEVIL

Will Phillips

Will Phillips has served in the Arizona State media relations department since 1995 and is a veteran of the U.S. Navy. He served from 1986 to 1991, and he was in the Middle East during Desert Storm.

A lot of people knew about Pat and what he did. They lost a friend. I also lost another soldier, in my mind, another great person that served our country, somebody that's been there and done that and has been under the fire. It was difficult when I first heard it just because I knew what he was doing.

When he did do this, it didn't surprise me that he wasn't just going to go in; he was going to be a Ranger. The guys in special operations are just a unique breed. I dealt with several SEALS units, did a bunch of stuff with frog guys, demolition guys, it's rough, but I understand that's what he wanted to do. When you're in these special branches, you're right there, you're not messing around.

I had a music appreciation class with him, one of those electives you have to take to get certain credits. It was a summer class in a big auditorium with 200 or 300 kids. That was about 1995, when I first met him. I'd see him way down in the front row, and I'd think, There's Pat sitting right down in front, right in front of teacher. Not many kids sit in front. He was sitting down there, his book wide open, just wide open. He wanted to be down in front, soak it all in, get in and get out. There wasn't a whole lot of messing around.

When I got to know him more, I just appreciated him more; the free spirit, he was just totally funny.

Whenever he came into the office, you knew he was there, good or bad. He was like a magnet. You wanted to be with him. You wanted to be engaged. He was such a goofball. So when he went into the service, I first thought that was really interesting. My second thought was, "Well, he's going to be a Ranger. That figures."

There wasn't any mincing of words. Whatever he said, that was him.

He was just a madman on the field. He was a heat-seeking missile. He was so intense. I remember the first time I started being a student intern, arranging interviews on the practice football field. I went to get Pat, and I'm thinking, "Oh, God, I hope he doesn't drop an 'F bomb.'" So I go get him, say guys want to talk to him, he's like, "Okay, dude." I'm thinking," Just be good."

There wasn't any mincing of words. Whatever he said, that was him. Also, that's why so many people liked him, good or bad.

THE REASON LIGHTNING NEVER STRIKES TWICE IN THE SAME PLACE IS—IT DOESN'T HAVE TO!

Arthur Johnson

Arthur Johnson, 35 is the assistant athletic director for football operations at the University of Texas, and he was the assistant to the head coach at Arizona State University in Tillman's final two seasons at the university.

The best tribute I could give Pat is that you only had to say something once. If you had to repeat it to him again, you'd better say it the same way. He'd never call you out publicly but he'd get you one-on-one and say, "Hey, that's not what you said two or three days ago."

He was the epitome of a student-athlete, always on time, no class issues. He competed hard, never had any excuses and then was able to navigate in that locker room, being *the guy* in the locker room. He'd be the outstanding player in the game, and then try to ease out of the locker room to escape all the attention.

I remember when lightning struck at Camp Tontozona one year. Everybody was supposed to get up the hill to wait for it to end. Pat stays out there on the field. I was in charge of everybody at camp so I'm thinking, "Okay, I probably shouldn't have been the first one up the hill because there's Pat's crazed butt sitting out there cross-legged in one of those puddles." And I'm there trying to decide...Is he that damned crazy? That was Pat.

He was low-maintenance when it came to us doing our job.

I remember when we were going to the Sun Bowl in 1997. We were talking about how the school gets there, what the process is, if players are on their own. Pat was going to drive back to campus with friends and he was trying to justify why he should get mileage from San Jose.

He is still the most unique person I've been around when it comes to being a student-athlete and one hell of a football player.

"As a teammate he led by example. He was all about every play, whether it was practice or the game. He had an intensity you can't describe."
　　—JAKE PLUMMER, Denver Broncos Quarterback, a teammate at Arizona State and with the Arizona Cardinals.

As we all grieve for the loss suffered by Pat Tillman's family and, indeed, all of us, we need not grieve for him. We all have a purpose in life and a responsibility to contribute to the betterment of mankind.

One young gentleman said it all: "Pat Tillman has inspired me to become a better man, a better person." There is no greater legacy. May all men aspire to Pat's integrity and honor.

　　　　　　　　　　　　　　　　—CINDY HARMS, Phoenix

A WARRIOR FOR A BATTLE

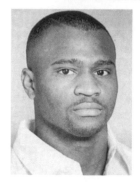

Terry Battle

Terry Battle played tailback at Arizona State University from 1994 to 1996.

P at and I came in together as freshmen in 1994. One of my greatest memories was freshman year at Camp Tontozona. Everybody is trying to take a nap between practices, but Pat is out there jumping off a cliff into the creek. We're like, "Oh, my goodness." He was one of those guys who lived his life to the fullest.

I didn't spend a lot of time with Pat in the dormitory setting. He would like to really focus in on schoolwork. I was more into football, and if I got a B or a C, I'd be happy. Pat was my hero in that respect—he did it both on the field and in the classroom.

Everyone really came into his own in 1996, the season ASU went to the Rose Bowl. We all matured. We all took our lumps the previous two years. A lot of us had to play early. That 1996 season, we knew we had something special with Pat. He really stepped up his game.

I struggled with how to practice hard. A lot of guys didn't want to practice hard. We were like, "It's too hot out there." Pat was like, "Guys, we've got full pads today. Let's go, let's go." He just left it all out on the practice field and the games.

YOU CAN'T SPELL PATRIOT WITHOUT P. A. T.

Bob Hobbs

Bob is one of the staunchest ASU athletic boosters, and has donated time and money to the building of the new ICA building. He travels with many teams, visits the athletic complex with some of it is named for him and has a keen interest in almost every athletic team. He is an ASU graduate of 1964.

I didn't know Pat real well, but I did know him. When we had the fiftieth anniversary of our company back in 1999, because of our extensive involvement with the ASU, we had a lot of athletes there. Pat was kind enough to come over even though this was done in the fall when football was going on. He was a solid guy and really a quiet guy. He might have been noisy on the football field. I wasn't out there with him then. He was a really bright guy. I'm sure he joined (the Army) because he felt he had a need to do something for his country. It's unfortunate that it ended in him giving his life for his country.

The Army Rangers, as I understand it, are just like the Navy SEALS—they're the toughest people we have, and they have to do the dirtiest work. You know he wasn't

John Madden lost his long-time partner after Super Bowl XXXVI when Pat Summerall retired. Pat Summerall's real first name is George. He is called Pat because when he was a kicker with the New York Giants football team, the newspapers would print: "P.A.T.-Summerall " P.A.T. stood for "Point After Touchdown." Summerall played minor league baseball against Mickey Mantle.

looking for anything except just being a true servant to his country, and being a protector. There aren't enough of those kinds of people around today, really.

When I first heard what Pat decided to do, I was frankly very proud of him. My thoughts are that many of our professional athletes are paid so much money they're out of touch with reality, not quite so much in football as in the other sports. I thought, "Here's a guy who's going to make a stand and do what he thinks is right." I'm a big admirer of Barry Goldwater, and that's the way Barry always operated. I like to feel like I operate that way. I'm a little old to join the service, but...I was very disappointed that he died. That's just all part of the risk of getting involved like that. The Rangers and SEALS are the guys who are going to be sent in whenever things are nasty. I have to tell you—I was not shocked when that happened. He marches to his own drumbeat. He was just an incredible guy, and I know he would not want to have a lot of attention paid to him now.

People I talked to when Pat first went in just kind of looked at you and said, "Well, that's Pat." I had dinner with Gene Smith last night, and he was saying, "Pat used to climb up on the tower at the stadium just so he could see what it looked like from up there." He danced to his own drummer. He had to be a really bright guy, first of all, to get a degree in marketing in three and a half years with a 3.8 grade average. For a normal student that's not playing football, that would be a hell of an accomplishment. Most people today take about five years to get out, and he did it in three and a half. He was just an unbelievable guy. He was a man's man and a patriot—and this country needs more patriots.

IF YOUTH KNEW, IF AGE COULD DO

Keith Poole

Keith Poole was a good friend of Pat's, and he was the star wide receiver on ASU's 1996 Rose Bowl team; he also was quarterback Jake Plummer's favorite target. He and Pat played together four years, and became fast friends. Both went on to the NFL, Poole with the New Orleans Saints and Denver Broncos, and always renewed their acquaintance before games each time their teams met.

When I heard Pat died, I talked to my wife quite a bit about it. Obviously, a lot of my memories about Pat were on the football field or at the clubs we'd frequent from time to time—going out and having a good time with the guys. All the stories about him are great, and what everyone is saying about him is so true. It's not just one of those deals where they're making stuff up and saying he's the greatest guy ever. He was. It's unbelievable the things he did.

One example was when we were at ASU and his girlfriend, now his wife, Marie, was back home. We'd win a game and, of course, we all were going to go out and party it up. Nearly every time Pat would say he had to be home by 10 p.m., because Marie was going to call him at his apartment. We'd say, "Come on, don't give us that." But he'd say, "No." He told her he'd be home by 10, so he would go home and wait for her call. It's just little things like that I remember. And as small a story as this is, it just shows his loyalty. We'd have fifteen guys, and we'd just beaten Nebraska, or whatever, and we'd want to go party, but he told his girlfriend he'd be home for a phone call—and he'd go home.

Back in those days I didn't really appreciate all of that. It was like, Pat, "We want you out. You're a fun guy." And now, looking back, you really appreciate his loyalty.

He was all business, and he was his own person. He didn't care what you thought about him. He didn't care what we thought about him because we'd call him every name in the book when he'd go home and wait for that phone call, but Pat was someone who was always thinking ahead. We were always thinking about "right now," all of us, "What can we do now?" But not him, he was thinking about school, football, his girlfriend. He would give coaches lists of players they should recruit. "We need to recruit these guys," he'd tell them, "We need this guy, we need a running back, we need another receiver," stuff like that. The rest of us would never even think about something like that—that's the coaches' job. Let's go worry about working out and playing.

He was just so intelligent. I talked to his dad at the Friday night get-together, one-on-one, for about fifteen minutes. I told him he needed to write a book on how to raise children. No one's perfect, but Pat was darned near. He was good-looking, a great athlete who had great morals, and he was a brilliant student. He was dedicated in every way. He was so much more mature than any other college kid could ever be. He was just above and beyond, and it's sad it had to end this way. I feel so blessed my daughter is going to be able to read about him in books. He was my teammate…he was my good friend…I'll get to tell her about him. Pat is going to make us all better people. He has already done that, because we all won't take so many things for granted. He truly was a great person.

I knew Kevin, Pat's brother, a little. I saw him play baseball at ASU, and I saw him hit his first home run. All those kids, including younger brother, Richard, are great. The parents did a great job raising them.

The last time I saw Pat was quite a while ago; I'm not even sure what the date was, but it was in 2001, when I was with the Saints we played the Cardinals. And no, I don't remember ever going over the middle for a pass. He never tackled me, but then again we didn't throw the ball much anyway. We played a little catch-up out on the field before that game. That was one of the last times I ever saw him. We spent some quality time together in the short time we could. But, I never went over the middle against him, and thank goodness for that! He probably would not have taken it easy on me.

Pat talked to my brother, Marc, who is paralyzed from the chest down due to an automobile accident he was in a few years ago. Marc, who was one of the 1996 Rose Bowl team's main inspirations, talked to Pat a lot more than I got to talk to him. Marc even talked to him a short time before this happened. They wrote letters to each other and talked on the phone, more than I got a chance to the past few years. A lot of guys on the team knew Marc, but Pat was the one guy who called him consistently. He never wanted any attention over darned near anything he did, and now he's getting it.

People asked me, when he went into the Army, "What is he doing? Is he crazy?" I told them that if they knew him, they wouldn't think that, because that's who he was. I laughed about it. He just excelled in everything he did.

IF TILLMAN WAS SUCH AN UNSELFISH PLAYER, WHY DID HE CARE ABOUT STATS?

Phil Snow

Phil was ASU's secondary coach until 1996 when he became its defensive coordinator during the school's Rose Bowl year. He knew Pat very well because he coached him. Pat liked to help Phil coach the defense, and many times did—during the games. Phil was also the Defensive Coordinator in 1997 when Tillman was named the Pac-10's defensive player of the year.

When I first heard about Pat, I always knew in the back of my mind that could happen. The first time he was over there, I would wake up every morning and hope there wasn't anything about Pat in the news. But when they tell you, well, it was a shock. It is a tragedy. Pat knew the ramifications of being in the military, but that is what he wanted to do and you have to respect that.

The last time I saw him was in June when he was stationed in Tacoma. He came up and visited one day. My thoughts go out to Pat's wife and his mom and dad. I think he and Marie had been dating for a long time. It's amazing to me how many people Pat touched in twenty-seven years. One day Pat came up here and went to lunch with Steve Emtman, UW's national Defensive Player of the Year in 1991. I'll bet when Steve heard the news he was really saddened. That's just the way Pat was. He touched a lot of people. He was really special, and a very unique guy.

Pat was a lot of things as a person. He was a tough, good-looking guy. He was extremely competitive. You know there is a saying with older people: He was a man's man. You always knew where you stood with Pat. There was no phoniness to him. He was always straightforward with you and wanted you to be straightforward with him. He was just a fantastic guy to be around. I was with him in bad situations, and in good, so I saw Pat in just about every light. He was just a terrific guy to be around.

I was with Pat four years and almost every story about him was great and true. I'll give you one of my favorites to show his passion for what he was doing. We were playing **Miami** in 1997 in the Orange Bowl, and Jeremy Staat had jumped offside for the sixth time. We stopped him, told him to cut it out and Coach Bruce Snyder was chewing defensive line coach Kevin Wolthausen's butt. Like he was going to do anything about it, right?

So the defense stopped them, and Pat storms off the field after Jeremy had jumped offside again. He came up to me and screamed, "Has anybody talked to Jeremy?" I said, "We all have. Now why don't you go try?" He said, "I will,'" and he marched off. I never knew whether or not he found Jeremy to scream at him. There are just so many stories on Pat.

He was the Pac-10 defensive player of the year in 1997, and it was richly deserved. He was the best defensive player in the conference that year. He earned it—and this from a 5-foot-10, 200-pound linebacker!

> **Do you confuse Miami (Ohio) with Miami (Florida)?**
> **Miami of Ohio was a school before Florida was a state.**

PHOENIX IS KNOWN AS "THE VALLEY OF THE SUN." IN THE SUMMER, IT SHOULD BE CALLED "THE SURFACE OF THE SUN."

Tom Sadler

Tom Sadler, 43, was an assistant athletic director for stadium management at ASU from 1988 until 2002. He is currently the associate athletic director for administrative services at the University of Hawaii.

After he left ASU, he got a nice contract with the Cardinals, and I'd see him riding his bike in south Tempe with a couple of movies in a shopping bag. He wouldn't drive his car—he'd ride his bike. It was the middle of the summer. I'd say, "Jeez, Pat."

I was at Camp Tontozona, and it was the end-of-camp scrimmage in 1994. I remember seeing this undersized defensive back-linebacker lay out a

> **He wouldn't drive his car—he'd ride his bike.**

tight end. I thought to myself at that moment, I've got to meet this kid because I've never seen what he was able to accomplish with his body size. He laid the tight end out and the tight end was twice his size—and he was nearly unconscious.

I've seen a lot of players come through Camp Tontozona, but he's the one I remember. There was something about his size and the way he went about playing. You just sensed something.

Working at the stadium, Sun Devil Stadium, with the Cardinals, he always seemed to be one of the first guys on the field on Sundays to work out before the game.

There's not another person I can even compare to him in terms of what he did with his life. Even before the military, it was mind-boggling the way he walked to the beat of his own drum.

As the stadium manager, I was shocked to learn he had been climbing the light towers to meditate. There was a photo of him up there in *Sports Illustrated*. I didn't even know he had been going up there.

...don't think I won't cite him as the epitome of a student athlete.

As I continue my career in athletic administration, don't think I won't cite him as the epitome of a student athlete.

I always felt Pat wasn't going to be one of the guys killed. I said, "There's no way." It didn't even cross my mind. I thought he was indestructible.

MOST BOWLERS ARE STEROID FREE

Harlen Rashada

Harlen Rashada, 29, was a teammate of Tillman's at Arizona State University in 1994 and 1995.

I do recall Pat very vividly. From the minute he got to ASU he was a stand-up guy. His character was just explosive. We always knew that.

I talked to Pat for about 90 minutes at Jake Plummer's celebrity bowling tournament. We just really had a good heart-to-heart conversation talking about life outside of football. My whole thing was, "Man, we all have to go through that." He genuinely listened to me. He really understood where I was coming from and knew that at some point that would have to be something he'd have to look at, too. He talked about the Cardinals briefly. He said, "I don't even know if I'm going to have a team to play for when I come back." He talked about his wife. He remembered me as a player, some of the things I did. Really, it was mostly about life. When it was over, I knew even more he was a stand-up guy.

I remember in his freshman picture, he had these little curly lock things coming down from his hair. It was more of a shag thing. I remember him coming in. He was a pretty strong dude. He ran well, and he played with a lot of heart, but it was in the meeting rooms where he'd trick you out. He'd be in meeting and we're all just tight in there trying to get it all down and he's like, "Yeah, dude, you know, dude this and dude that to the coaches. We're like, "Whoa man, you can't talk to them like that." But that's just how he was. He was easygoing and free-spirited.

You knew what you got with Pat. He was accountable. Pat was kind of a quite assassin on the field. He was one of those guys you could look in his face and feel his intensity. He didn't have to yell a lot or be vocal. He led by his actions. But you never doubted for one minute in the locker room that No. 42 was a guy who was going to go out and give it his all. You knew what you got with Pat. He was accountable.

Pat Tillman proves that the greatest generation never stops with one generation in America.
—SCOTT SPENCER, Black Canyon City, AZ

Pat Tillman is the Nathan Hale, Sgt. York and Audie Murphy for this time in American history.
—CAROLYN NELSON, Sun City West, AZ

THE ROSE BOWL...
OR AS THEY CALL IT IN TUCSON,
PASSOVER

Tim Healy

Tim is Arizona State University's radio play-by-play man, and during Pat's playing career at ASU was a sportscaster for Channel 3 in Phoenix. He has followed Pat's career closely, both at ASU and as a Phoenix Cardinal.

In my opinion, the best way to describe Pat Tillman is that he's almost like peeling a piece of fruit that has a whole bunch of layers to it.

You peel down one layer, and you get the macho athlete, the tough guy.

Then you peel away another layer, and you get the intellectual who graduated college in three and a half years with outstanding grades.

Then you peel another layer, and there's the real compassionate guy who sometimes is more interested in what you're doing than in what he's doing.

Then you peel another layer, and you get just kind of a California surfer dude.

In fact, one of my fond remembrances is that during the Rose Bowl year, he came out to do one of the weekly interviews late in the season. It became obvious at this point that we were probably going to be heading to the Rose Bowl. I asked, "Hey, Pat, what do you think it will be like playing in Pasadena on New Years Day. You would figure to get some kind of jock speak or whatever. He just looked at me and said, "Man, that would be way cool!" I don't think I had ever heard playing in the Rose Bowl described in those terms.

The thing that makes me emotional about Pat is how much my son admires him. I have a twenty-one-year-old son who's a junior here at ASU. For Christmas a couple of years ago, I got him a Cardinals number 40 jersey. The day Pat was killed, the day the news came out, he started wearing it and has worn it a lot since. When I go in, and he's still signed on to the computer, there's a screensaver of Pat in his number 40, helmet in hand, screaming something, probably with an expletive mixed in there somewhere. It really impacts me to mourn the passing and to celebrate the life of a guy that impacts my son. That's probably the best memory I have of him.

My overwhelming memory is that the guy was so much— so many layers—a special guy. How many of us have the convictions he did, and then to act on them the way he did. I've never been prouder to be associated with Arizona State. The ideals that Pat lived for, personified, died for, reflect well on all Sun Devils.

When you really think about it, in that month, some of the most significant stories in America—Phil Mickelson winning the Masters, Barry Bonds with home runs flying, and now, Pat Tillman—certainly offer different dynamics and dimensions.

DENVER = OMAHA
WITH MOUNTAINS

Matt English

Matt English grew up in a small town in Vermont, attending a high school that didn't have a football team. His parents moved to Phoenix a couple years after Matt graduated from high school, and Matt followed, enrolling at Arizona State. His first experience with football came during 1996 as a student trainer at ASU. Currently, Matt lives in Denver where he is a certified athletic trainer with HealthOne.

The first time I saw Pat was at Camp Tontozona, Arizona State's training camp. He was a small guy for a linebacker but he seemed bigger than life...certainly bigger than his stature. Although he was quiet, he had a big, booming voice.

I remember the first time I saw him, he was walking down to practice, with long hair and looked really physically fit. He looked like an animal. Opponents probably felt that way. He always gave 110 percent.

As an athletic trainer, I interacted with all the guys on the team. That year, 1996, Pat didn't seem to be injured at all. Still, he was a really nice guy and very thankful for any help we gave him. He seemed to be well-liked by the rest of the team and the coaches. I've had the privilege of working with the Denver Broncos a little bit. There's a big sign framed on the wall in the training room that states: "You can always judge the character of a man by how he treats someone who can do nothing for him." That was Pat. He would talk to anyone. He was a nice guy. He was always thankful regardless of how minute the gesture that he received. He was that type of guy.

When Pat left the NFL to join the Army, it was hard to believe but it wasn't shocking. If there was any one guy from that Arizona State team who would do that, it would be Pat. It was a shock that he turned down millions of dollars to go fight for his country. That is so honorable. I think all of us, particularly those who haven't served in the military, could relate to the thought of having not done anything, as Pat stated when he joined the Army. But most of us don't do anything about it. I could relate to that personally.

> **If I had a chance, I would like to personally thank him for the sacrifice he made.**

I think Pat was one of those guys who was very approachable, even if you didn't know him very well. You almost as if you were his friend, even after meeting him one time. That's an awesome trait for anyone to have.

If I had a chance, I would like to personally thank him for the sacrifice he made. Or, at least personally thank his family and his wife for the sacrifice that he made to go out and protect our country.

He's definitely an inspiration. I have a 14-month-old boy, and we went to Tempe recently and looked at the memorial outside Sun Devil Stadium. It was so powerful to see things that people left behind. I'm glad I could go and take my son. He definitely will know the story of Pat Tillman when he's old enough to understand it.

THE REASON SOME PEOPLE ARE ARIZONA WILDCAT FANS IS BECAUSE THEY CAN'T AFFORD ROSE BOWL TICKETS

Vince D'Aliesio

Vince D'Aliesio was a graduate assistant offensive line coach during Pat Tillman's time at Arizona State. After leaving ASU in 1997, D'Aliesio moved to Southern California and helped coach at the high school level. Currently living in Clovis, Calif., D'Aliesio is an insurance agent.

It really hit me hard when I heard the news of Pat's death. It's been a somber time, because Pat was "every man." He was the guy that you'd never thought something like this would happen to. When we found out he was joining the military, it was odd because he did his own thing. He drummed to his own beat, but it was something that was bound to happen because he was the consummate team player.

The first time I met Pat was in the spring of 1995 when I first started working with Arizona State. It was just a hello meeting in study hall late at night. Usually when the freshmen would gather there, they'd laugh and joke around. But Pat was there studying. He wasn't the type of person to go out of his way to introduce himself, but he was a remarkable person. He just did his job.

I was the assistant offensive line coach, a graduate assistant, so I didn't interact directly with Pat that often. But when we were around each other, he was very respectful. I'd see him up at mandatory study hall late at night after spring practice and he was very respectful. And he was always studying.

One incident that stuck out in particular was when we were getting ready to play the University of Arizona, Arizona State's archrival, in 1996, my second year there. Every time we had a great season, they would come along and be the spoiler, and vice versa. We were getting ready for a team meeting about two hours before kickoff. Everything was quiet. Earlier in the day, Ohio State and Michigan had played. OSU, like us, was 10-0 going into that game. Ohio State and ASU had received a Rose Bowl bid the week before. Michigan upset Ohio State. So, the Buckeyes were going to the Rose Bowl at 10-1. We were sitting around the meeting room at the hotel, waiting to get started. All of a sudden, a guy came into the meeting room whistling. It took a few seconds before we realized it was Pat, and he was whistling the Michigan fight song. It kind of loosened things up. It was a reminder that we were getting ready to play Arizona, a team that hadn't played that well, but a team that could upset us. Pat was sending everyone a message that we could just as easily lose as Ohio State had earlier. Well, sure enough, we went on to beat Arizona 56-14, and went undefeated. We beat the hell out of them on both sides of the ball. We would have had two more scores but they were called back because of penalties. We had already sealed our bowl berth, so there was no reason we should have done as well as we did. Many teams would have rested on their laurels that night, but we didn't. If Pat were around today, he probably wouldn't remember whistling that song. That was my best memory of Pat Tillman.

Pat never wanted to host recruits. He thought the whole process was a farce. He figured that if a kid wanted to go to a school, he should go. He hated hosting recruits. But certain players would be requested more than others. Jake Plummer, Keith Poole and Juan Roque were some of the popular ones, as well as Pat. He always said an emphatic no, though. During recruiting in the spring of 1997, Pat's junior year, we told him that we absolutely needed him to do it to help bring in a solid recruiting class. The way it worked, we would take the recruits to a local restaurant the first night, and the host would usually meet us there. Then, the recruit and his host player would leave and have a good time. We told Pat to meet us at the restaurant on this particular Friday evening. We got there with the recruits, and Pat was there with one of his teammates. They had gotten there early. Pat happened to have a couple empty beer bottles in front of him. That was the last time he hosted a recruit, at least while I was there.

> **Pat wasn't a loud leader, he led by his actions. He danced to his own beat**

Pat wasn't a loud leader, he led by his actions. He danced to his own beat. I don't remember if Pat was an avid surfer, but under his shoulder pads he wore a wet suit. This was before that apparel Under Armour came out. He was the first and only guy I had ever seen wear a wet suit. From our seasons in 1996 and '97 you can kind of see it in team pictures. Pat did everything his own way, but it was within the structure of the team. I don't remember Pat being a team captain, but there was a lot of respect for Pat Tillman. People would want to be like Pat as a leader, but he wouldn't want that designation. I don't know that he would want that responsibility. He got the job done. He was a dynamic person.

On the field, he always had a habit of being around the ball. Specific plays didn't stand out, but he was always around the ball. His sophomore year I remember that he was a part-time starter. He established himself the next year. When Pat was a junior we had a guy walk-on. Then, when Pat left, Adam Archuleta took over Pat's spot. Ironically, when Pat didn't go to the St. Louis Rams, it gave the Rams a need to draft Adam and allowed him to start as a rookie.

We should all be so lucky to do all that Pat was able to do. Death is very hard and sad, but what a way to go. To be adored by as many people as he was. For a guy who just wanted to do his own thing and be respected, it's something to be a Patriot and a hero. I can't say enough great things about him.

I was in the same recruiting class as Pat and we played together all four years. I'm wearing #42 on my Rattlers helmet and the rest of the Rattlers are wearing #40, Pat's Cardinal number. I've got 42 on there because that's how I knew him at ASU. We were close, but he wouldn't hesitate to yell at me if he thought I needed it. One time we got into a fight in practice. Afterwards we were laughing about it because that's how intense we were.

—**VINCE AMEY**, Arizona Rattlers of the Arena Football League

A SUMMER CAMP NAMED TONTOZONA...OOOH, THAT SOUNDS LIKE FUN

Bruce Snyder

Snyder is one of the greatest Arizona State University coaches ever, leading the Sun Devils to an undefeated 1996 regular season (11-0) and a 1997 Rose Bowl berth opposite Ohio State.

I almost naively had a sense that the guy was inde-structible and invincible—he was so smart and so athletic and so courageous that he would be fine. Obviously, war is a difficult thing, and those things don't hold up.

I bet right from the time he was a youngster, he was on the ground running. He made decisions about what he was going to do in life that were clear to him. I feel grate-ful I had the chance to know him. He cut a wide swath. I admire the dog out of him.

Everybody you run into, the person on the street, the guy at the barber shop, every high school student asks, "What was Pat really like?" and "What are the feelings?" On the bottom line of it, I feel very blessed that I had a chance to be with Pat, and I learned more from him than he learned from me.

When he arrived in '94, he came with all the equip-ment—the really important stuff. I'd like to take some credit for it, but I can't—and shouldn't. He came with integrity, intelligence, principles—he was charismatic. His family did a great job with him.

I just tried to keep him on the team and keep the team moving forward. I'll miss him a great deal. I cannot tell you how many times I've been sitting around on a sofa with friends, and a Tillman story would pop up. It was like, "Let me tell you about this one," and I would start smiling. This was over the last four or five years, not just since he died.

We knew he was remarkable when we had him. It was like, "This guy's special." I don't know if I did a good job of explaining it, but there was a love affair. I happened to be the matchmaker—that this guy ought to be on our team. In fact, I needed him on the team. It wasn't just a nice idea. The Valley fell in love with him. He really loved Arizona State. He loved Tempe. He loved Phoenix, and the state of Arizona. It was a terrific love affair appreciated by both sides. I think both sides got a lot out of the relationship.

That's why we're grieving so much. It's the end of a romance. That's sad.

There are a lot of Tillman stories. My favorite, at any given time, depends on the environment I'm in and what message I want to get across. If you document all of them, there are things for every part of your life—anything that might come up I think there's a story.

There was the time he told me, "I'm not red-shirting." At the time, I went, "Oh, really?" This occurred over lunch. Then before he finished his soup, he followed that up with, "Oh, by the way, I'll start by the end of the season." I went back to my staff room and said, "Hey, guys, I've got to tell you this conversation I just had. This is really something—this young, hippie dude, this super dude."

The staff members all remembered my coming back in and saying that, "Here's this guy who doesn't understand how hard Division I football is," and thinking how wise I was. Well, by the end of the season, he was starting on a lot of units. Life was not a red-shirt option for him.

He didn't live long, and that's sad, but the guy cut a wide path. I think that's all we can really hope for in our lives.

Money was not an issue with Pat. In his mind, it would be easy to be rich.

> **He didn't live long...but the guy cut a wide path.**

Obviously, Sun Devil Stadium brings back some very fond memories for me personally. In 1994 a love affair began, an unlikely love affair, maybe like many love affairs are unlikely. But here was a young man, long hair, jeans, flip-flops on his feet and a community that was looking for heroes and people to cheer for.

I've watched it not only through Pat's four years with Arizona State but his career with the Cardinals. I go back to the genesis of this and that would be a setting at Tontozona—a nice, rustic place to spend about ten days in August. I had lunch with Pat along with some other freshmen, and I mentioned he might want to think about red-shirting that year. Red-shirting is an NCAA term for sitting out a year of competition. Maturing, growing, learning so you're better able to compete. In a broader sense, and I think it was the start of this attention towards Pat, he said, "No, coach, I am not red-shirting. I want to graduate in four years. I have things to do with my life." I really believe what he meant was, life does not include a red-shirt. It doesn't have one of those. Life is not a dress rehearsal. That's what he was talking about.

That showed in the way he played. The fans I knew in the stands here started watching this young man and said, "This guy knows how to play the game." And he was that way his entire career here, both on and off the field. He never missed a class, he never missed a practice. I don't know if he ever missed a tackle. There was no red-shirt in Pat Tillman's life. I think we all appreciate that in him very much. We want to make sure, and I'm probably talking about myself mostly here, we take something positive from Pat's life.

One of the responsibilities of a coach is to go out and recruit. Of course, at UNLV I'm looking for another Pat Tillman. But what is the most encouraging for me is I've been in forty high schools, ten junior colleges and a lot of states in the West, and I would venture there isn't a coach who doesn't talk to his team he currently has about the values and the life of Pat Tillman. You think about it for a moment, and that's a huge number who are listening in their growing and developmental states about how to live your life. And we have here a living person who showed us how to do it.

I think we have a world of young people, and by God our country needs young people who will be leaders in about fifteen, twenty years. We need good leaders, principled leaders and I think about a number of them coming in the system now that will have benefited directly by the life of Pat Tillman. When I tell Pat Tillman stories, which I have done the last four, five years, I always smile—either on my face or in my heart. And I would like for all of you to feel the same. And I'm sure many of you do. The legacy of Pat Tillman would be to go out, be bold, be courageous and act upon your beliefs. In my 40 years of coaching you run across all kinds of young people. He is the most unique of them all.

God bless Pat Tillman.

"In today's world of instant gratification and selfishness, here is a man who was defined by words like loyalty, honor, passion, courage, strength and nobility."
—**BOB FERGUSON,** Seattle Seahawks General Manager

ISN'T MINNESOTA MENTIONED IN THE BIBLE..."MANY ARE COLD BUT FEW ARE FROZEN?

Jason Verdugo

Verdugo was Jake Plummer's backup at quarterback for two years before Jason decided to play baseball for ASU. He wound up playing professionally, later taking a job with Hamline University in St. Paul, Minn., as its baseball coach and assistant athletic director. Jason played with Pat for two years at Arizona State University, and is a very perceptive young man—noticing many things about Pat.

There isn't a person who played with him who didn't like him, obviously, or respect him. I played with him for two years, and I played one year with Kevin on the baseball team. Kevin was a little different than Pat, but to be honest they were very, very similar. It was almost like playing with the same guy at times.

It was a joy to play with him. He was an unbelievable talent. The main thing I'll remember most, and first impressions are everything, was his image. On one of our first scrimmages at camp, he took on fullback Jeff Paulk, a 250-pounder who was drafted by Atlanta in the fourth round of the NFL draft. It was an unbelievable collision. Guys had their eyes opened when that hit occurred. Later that evening, he was in the cafeteria, sitting by himself, reading a book, and drinking coffee. I mean who the hell brings books to camp *and reads them*? And I had never seen an eighteen-year-old drink coffee. Maybe it was we who were different, and he was the one who was normal.

He was really all business. Just knowing him made me a better person, I'll tell you that. I think a lot of people would say the same thing. I was with him for about four days at a camp in Colorado, and he still had the same motivation, and the same quietness he had when we played. He was great with the kids. They flocked to him every day. He was the kids' world for those four days, and they were his world. He loved them and they loved him. He busted his butt for them.

I was on the golf course when I heard about his death. A friend called me on my cell phone and said he had some bad news. I was devastated and shocked. I would love to see the NFL buck up and put their money where their mouth is by giving Marie something. His family deserves it.

I remember Pat going to Camp Tontozona and reading books. He was a different character. One of my assistants, Eddie Zube, was a walk-on, junior-college transfer from Northern California at ASU. On the first day of spring practice, he was sitting on the sidelines putting his shoes on, and Pat came up and told him, "I hear you're from the Bay Area, too. If there's anything you need, let me know, and I'll help you get it." That's the kind of guy he was.

I know he loved ASU. The fans loved him because he always busted his ass on the football field. He had a good time with them. He never wanted any attention, but he always seemed to have time for the fans. When he ran an interception back for a touchdown with the Cardinals, he never danced. He just tossed the ball to the referee. He just thought that was part of his job.

—STEVE CAMPBELL, Third-team Quarterback with Tillman at
    ASU, now head coach at Tempe McClintock High School

We were in a playoff game, and at the half we were leading 55-0. There was a running clock going on to make it easier and to get the game over with. As we went back on the field for the second half, I went up to Pat and said, "Pat, you're done for the day. I don't want you playing any offense or defense." He looked at me and said, "OK." As we were getting prepared for the second half kickoff, my offensive coordinator said to me, "You know Pat's back there ready to take the kickoff." I looked in astonishment and saw him back there. He got the kickoff, and, of course, ran it back for a touchdown. As he came off the field, he came up to me very confidently and said, "You mentioned nothing about special teams." He was right, and so we wouldn't have any more misinterpretation about words, we claimed his helmet and shoulder pads.

When he was a freshman in high school, he tried out for the baseball team. He wanted to play varsity baseball. Pat was a catcher. He was really undersized. I worked with him quite a bit and the final decision came down that he was not going to make the varsity baseball team. He was cut from the **varsity**, and he was going to be on the frosh team. He was not happy with that. He wanted to quit baseball at that point in time. I said, "I really wish you wouldn't do that because I think you'd have a great opportunity and a great future in baseball." He said, "No, Coach. I'm going to get in the weight room tomorrow and become a football player. I said, in my wisdom, "Pat, that's probably a bad decision, because if you're going to play a college sport, it's going to have to be baseball. It can't be football."

—TERRY HARDTKE, Pat Tillman's coach at Leland High School, San Jose, CA

The word "varsity" is the British short form of the word "university."

Pat Tillman was the kind of kid that the game of football is all about, but particularly at the college level. You wonder how he could make it at the pro level, but he did because of his sheer perseverance and determination, even though he was an undersized kid. At the collegiate level, he was a great example of what can be done with limitations—speed, athletic ability, size—but with desire and determination.

He was a leader, but the intriguing thing about him was that he perpetuated leadership by his actions. I think he died the way he lived. He was a very bright guy. I knew a couple of his faculty members, and they said he was always prepared. He played football the same way.

We spoke a few times, although I didn't know him intimately well, and I could see the dedication and perseverance. Pat was the type of guy that any coach would want on his team, whether it's college or any other level.

He felt the same about his family as he did the guys he played with. He was a great citizen and he had a great deal of personal pride, along with a great attitude and dedication. All of those were his premiere factors. Because of his knowledge and his dedication, this is a great loss to our society, there's no question about it. He potentially would have been the kind of guy who could've run for a political office and been a great addition to our country.

—FRANK KUSH, the Greatest Sun Devil of them all

Chapter 3

The Big Red, White and Déja Blue

Experience is What You Get When You Don't Get What You Want

BIG BIRD

Michael Bidwill

Michael is a son of Cardinals owner Bill Bidwill, and is currently the team's vice president and general counsel. Michael was touched greatly by Pat's decision to join the U.S. Army, and much admired him for his decision. Michael has been the team's spokesman of late, and was superb at a memorial for Pat at Sun Devil Stadium.

I had read about Pat when he was playing at ASU that he was part surfer-boy from California, excellent athlete, over-achiever, and bright guy—a guy who was a little bit different. When he came here, and we got to know him, you realized he was a really special person. He was very bright, very thoughtful, determined. He had uncommon determination and when he made up his mind, he would get it done. He didn't care what people had to say. People had said he wasn't big enough to play linebacker in college. They said he wasn't fast enough to play any position in the NFL, and we switched him to safety. What occurred was that he took a starting position, and then a year or two later, he not only had the starting position, but broke a team record that had stood for many, many years. I think we learned more about him and his character and determination when he came back and told us that it was time for him to step away from football and go play for a bigger team than an **NFL** team—the Army Rangers.

Twenty years ago, two-thirds of all NFL field goals were made. Now, better than 80 percent are successful.

I wasn't particularly shocked about his decision. There was a part of me that knew that every off-season; he would do something that was way different than anybody thought. Nothing had happened that year except we did know that he was going to marry Marie. Marie was his high school sweetheart who he had stayed true to throughout all of his time in Arizona. That's a special thing in and of itself.

Everybody's first reaction to his enlistment was, "He's doing what?" When I initially heard it, I thought, "Well, he's going to do it. There's no talking him out of it." It had nothing to do with money or anything else. He was just going to do this, and that's what he was going to do, and the whole thought was, "Well, let's keep his jersey to the side and not let anybody else wear it, because we'd like to have him back in a few years if he's ready to return to football." I thought the thing that was particularly special was not just walking away from a substantial amount of money, but I think the year before he had been given a bigger offer from the Rams and decided to stay with the Cardinals because we were the ones who drafted him—he had his loyalty to us. That was another part of Pat.

Probably the most significant thing about his death is his settling down with his high-school sweetheart. He'd gotten married. He's back after his honeymoon. Then just a few weeks later, he and Kevin together are going to join the Army. There are very few people, if any, who would walk away from three and a half million dollars. Then you compound that with walking away from the three and a half million dollars AND the love of his life whom he had just married. There's nobody except for Pat Tillman who would do both those things.

When we played the Giants at the **Meadowlands** in December 2001, we set up a visit down to Ground Zero and to one of the fire stations. Pat was particularly focused on that day, inquisitive, thoughtful—appeared to be introspective, as well. He was asking a lot of questions of the policemen and firemen who were there giving us the tour.

In an interview after the tours, Pat said, "My grandfather was at Pearl Harbor, but what the hell have I done? I've done nothing." In hindsight and looking back, you could see what he was going through—he was really telling us all that his mind was starting to be made up that he needed to do something about this. He was certain, as was everybody, that on September 11, 2001, we got into a war, whether we liked it or not. And the U.S. government policy was going to be was to get the fight off our shores and to take it right to them in Afghanistan and Iraq and other places where these al Qaeda-friendly countries were allowing this to foster. You could see that he was just really moved by what he had seen—the amount of devastation that these people had inflicted on our country.

Pat Tillman always was a great American. You could see it in his eyes.

He made a decision sometime after September 11 that he was going to trade in his football cleats for Army boots and his football jersey for fatigues. He was going to play

> More NFL games have been played at the Meadowlands than at any other current ballpark or stadium. Wrigley Field held the record until halfway through the 2003 NFL season.

for America's team. He was going to give the same amount of heart that he gave on the football field for many years at Arizona State and for the Cardinals fans who watched as he played at Sun Devil Stadium and on TV. That's what we learned when we saw the reports about the **Silver Star**. That was just unbelievable. You can see him turning his group around and saying, "Let's get back over there and save those guys,"—leading the charge and giving his all, which he did. He gave his life!

We knew, when he joined the Army, he wasn't fooling around. It's no surprise to find out that he was his squad leader—because we knew that was always a leader. For him to be in the more-elite units and for him to rise to the top and be a leader is no surprise. He was brilliant. He was determined. He was loyal to his commanders and to his soldiers. He was a great soldier. Some of the people in his platoon described him in that same way.

When we were playing in Seattle last season, it was great to have him visit us. He was really relaxed, glad to be back on leave. He couldn't talk about what he was doing. We had a wonderful day watching the football game. He brought Kevin and Marie and some other friends. We all relaxed and had a lot of fun.

Pat Tillman, at the end of the day, was a great guy. He was a guy's guy. He loved to have fun. He loved to joke around. He was just Pat. He'd have a couple of beers and

The Silver Star is awarded to a person who, while serving in any capacity with the Army, is cited for gallantry in action against an enemy while engaged in military operations involving conflict with an opposing force.

a couple of hot dogs enjoying time with his family. He was very relaxed and glad to be up in our suite. He sent me a very nice note afterwards, with a photograph that we had taken together with my father-in-law. I found the photograph and am trying to find the note—I hope I didn't throw it away. It was short and sweet, basically saying, "Thanks." I feel so relieved that I got a chance to say goodbye to him.

You think about the number of times you hug the people in your family. In the last six months, I've hugged my mom and hugged my dad. I don't know that I've hugged any of my brothers. I know I've hugged my sister. But the one thing I did that day last December was I got a chance to hug Pat Tillman on the way in and hug him on the way out. I'm so grateful that I got that opportunity to look him in the eye and say, "Thank you."

In sports and in life, we overuse terms like courage, bravery and, hero. And then somebody special, really special, like Pat Tillman comes along and shows us what those words really mean, and it's humbling to know that he was here—that he was a part of Arizona, and Arizona State, and the Arizona Cardinals. What a great guy!

He was so incredibly loyal to the people he knew. He supported them and loved them, starting with his friends and family back in San Jose to his friends and teammates at Arizona State to his friends and teammates here with the Cardinals.

I was at home, and a friend called me and at that point, he thought it was only a rumor that either Pat or Kevin had been killed, and he didn't know if it was in combat or not. It felt like a kick to the gut. I was shocked. Then I turned on TV and saw that they were confirming it. Probably the hardest phone calls I had to make were the ones to my family to let them know what happened—waking up my father before seven a.m. and waking up my sister and others. Those are the phone calls you don't want to get. As it sunk it that he was killed in action, in combat, I thought, This is really hard stuff. But, you know what? We didn't start this stuff. I think that's what Pat recognized. These guys tried to give us a black eye on **9/11**, and Pat recognized it and said, "You know what. I'm going to trade in my cleats for some Army boots and go help out with this fight." What a great American!

When former Olympic gold medal figure skater Peggy Fleming was stranded in New York following the September 11th attacks, she hitched a ride to her San Francisco home on the Madden Cruiser, the custom bus that Madden travels in because of his fear of flying.

Pat was one of my favorite players. I used to hang with him a little after he graduated. He, Jake Plummer and I would go bowling, and we always had a good time. One of my favorite stories was when we were coming back from Sky Harbor on a bus after a great win in the Sun Bowl. All of a sudden we hear, "Hey, dude, stop the bus! Dude, stop the bus!" He took his girlfriend, Marie, who later became his wife, and they grabbed their knapsacks and simply got off the bus without telling anyone where they were going. He was different.

—*GREG WAILAITIS*, former Marketing Director, ASU

THESE 10 THINGS ARE THE 7 SIGNS THAT YOU'RE HOOKED ON TILLMAN

Dave McGinnis

Dave McGinnis, 52, was head coach of the Arizona Cardinals from the middle of the 2000 season to 2003, during Pat's tenure with the NFL team. They became close friends, and McGinnis also got to know Pat's wife, Marie, and his family. It was McGinnis who elevated Tillman to a starting position at safety after Pat had played special teams his rookie year. McGinnis knew the value of having Pat on the field—at all times. He's currently the associate head coach of the Tennessee Titans. McGinnis spoke at both of Tillman's memorial services and said that Tillman was one of his favorite players.

In the memorial ceremony in San Jose, a Navy SEAL who served with Pat in Iraq said that in 1976-2004, the dash represents a lot of living. Pat Tillman put everything into that dash. Pat Tillman lived life.

There will be very appropriate and fitting tributes not only for Pat Tillman, but for all of our young men and women who so greatly protect our freedoms and what we are able to do. Tillman was a very special, unique person. And, at the same time, all our young men and women serving over there are unique. The pain I'm feeling is felt throughout the country.

After Pat had decided to end his football playing and enter the military, Pat came into the office, pulled his chair around and said, "We need to talk." He went through it all. It was his wish that this not draw a lot of attention. He went into all the ramifications, all of what was going to happen. I said to him, "Pat, this will be quite the storm here. How do you propose to deal with it?" He said, "'Mac, I'm not going to. You are." When he finally sat me down to tell me he was joining the Army, there wasn't extreme shock. Everything he did, he thought out.

He didn't have a dial. He had a switch, and it was either on or off.

I'm going to cherish it that dinner we had in Seattle last year, and I am just so thankful for the time I knew him. I knew him not only as a coach but as a friend. We all knew he was very special. He had a real sense of commitment and integrity, plus he had passion and exuberance for everything he did. There was so much more to him than most. He had depth in every aspect of his life. I had gotten to know that person. I had seen that, been involved with that metamorphosis.

There have been countless requests for interviews since his death, and I feel I owe him that. He just puts a recognizable face and life on all those men and women over there. I'm sure every young man and woman over there has to be thinking about the possibility of dying, but the commitment to duty supersedes it.

Pat always shunned the limelight, and I am sure he would want that continued, but his life deserves to be celebrated and his story to be heard.

During the 2001 season, the Cardinals' kicker, Bill Gramatica, tore knee ligaments when, after making a field goal, he jumped high in the air and landed awkwardly. The trainer, John Omohundro, comes up to me to tell me about Bill, and Tillman comes up sprinting and pushes Johnny O aside. Pat said, "You know who's kicking, don't you?" I said, "Pat, can you do it?" He said, "Hell, yeah, I can do it. Hell, yeah." I said, "OK." He looked at me and said, "Cool."

Pat Tillman was honor, integrity, decency. Those weren't just adjectives in Pat Tillman's life. They were his life.

Pat Tillman was the embodiment of loyalty and commitment; I experienced those first-hand. When Larry Marmie and I worked Pat out before we drafted him, we were there on the practice field at Arizona State University. A fifteen-minute session turned into a forty-five minute ordeal because he wouldn't let us leave. He'd say, "Coach, you know damn well I can do better than that. So, let's do it again."

Pat had a chance to leave in free agency for a lot more money. I can remember him standing there in the weight room when he came back from his visit with the St. Louis Rams and saying, "I'm not going anywhere." In his words, "How could I leave the organization and the coaches who believed in me and gave me a chance? That wouldn't be fair."

The Rev. Dr. Martin Luther King, in one of his many addresses, said that the true measure of a man is not where he stands in times of comfort and convenience but where he stands in times of conflict. There was never a question of where Pat Tillman stood.

If you wanted his opinion all you had to do was ask him. And if you didn't want his opinion, he'd still give it to you.

Pat Tillman defined the word character.

On a December Saturday night in Seattle, before the Cardinals played the Seahawks last year, I was blessed to be in a hotel room with Pat, Kevin, Marie and Ben. I felt an overwhelming sense of pride. I was enthralled with what I was seeing—these young people, their passion, their energy, their love for one another.

Everyone felt like Pat belonged to them. I can still see us at training camp in Flagstaff, coming off the field, and the people surrounding No. 40 to get his autograph—the little kids, the grandmothers, the macho guy who wanted to be a linebacker, the young girls, the old girls—just because Pat Tillman was a man that invited everything.

The last words I ever said to Pat Tillman were "thank you" as he left our locker room.

See No. 42, Pat's ASU number. Now see No. 40, Pat's Cardinals number). Now close your eyes and picture your most valued and treasured Pat Tillman moment on this football field. I've got so many Pat Tillman moments, but three come to mind immediately.

In 1998, in the next-to-last game of the season, when we had to win every game down the stretch to go to the playoffs, he made a play right there at midfield that got us over the hump against the New Orleans Saints. In September 2000 he was all over this football field. He had seven tackles, three breakups in a 32-31 win over Dallas. In October 1999, and I can still see it, he had his very first NFL interception right there. He was someone every one of us coaches would want on our team.

Now I ask you, don't look anymore with your eyes, look with your heart. That lump you feel in your throat right now? That's Pat. Those tears in your eyes right now?

That's Pat. That sense of pride you feel welling up in your chest and wanting to burst out of every pore of your body? That's Pat. That's the gift he gave to us.

What a special gift it is from a very special man. The Prime Minister of England, during World War II, had this to say about his brave young men and women during that conflict. He said the legacy of a brave man is the memory of a great name and the inheritance of a great example. What a fabulous example we have in Pat Tillman.

I was stopped coming back from San Jose in the airport in Los Angeles by a woman who had watched the ceremonies. And as she approached me she said, 'Coach, I just want to introduce myself and tell you during those ceremonies I went into the other room and brought my 13-year-old son in and said, 'Watch this, hear this and listen to this. This is a man you want to know.' We all know limits begin where vision ends, and Pat Tillman had no limits because his vision wasn't just limited to his eyesight. He saw with his heart, he saw with his intellect, he saw with his emotions and most of all he saw with his honor.

In 500 B.C., Pericles was the commander of 100 men in the Greek Wars. He said of every 100 men, 10 will stay behind, 80 are there to receive orders, nine are real fighters, and we are lucky to have them, but one, ah, but one, will be a warrior. He will bring the others home. Pat Tillman has brought us all home. He brought us all home to the reality of the words honor, integrity, dignity, commitment.

The English essayist, Raymond Chandler, wrote these words: Down the mean streets a man must go who himself is not mean, who is neither tarnished nor afraid. He is a brave man. He is everything. He must be a complete man and a common man yet an unusual man. He must be, to use a rather weathered phrase, a man of honor by instinct, by inevitability, without thought of it and certainly without saying it. He must be the best man in his world, and a good enough man for any world.

We are all so thankful Pat Tillman is in our world. He will always be in our world. It is our duty to keep his spirit alive in our world.

So, in addition to the fear of death, the fear of pain, the fear of extreme discomfort, the fear of insolvency, and the fear of the unfamiliar, Pat Tillman somehow found the wherewithal in a mere 27-year lifetime to vanquish a fear even more pertinent in the day-to-day puzzle: the fear of what others might think.

He did so despite spending generous time in sports-team locker rooms, bastions of pack mentality and of stringent behavioral codes.

It's astounding.

All hail to the soldier, yes, and all hail to the volunteer, and all hail to the volunteer, and all hail to the fallen who died in southeastern Afghanistan trying to ensure no other dates would match September 11 for poignancy.

But let's try to remember one aspect that made the heart plunge into the gut when the news flashed: All hail to the "eccentric."

All hail to the "flake" to the devotee of the alleged "different drummer," to the unconventional. We don't have enough courage of conviction running around not to bemoan when we lost it.

—CHUCK CULPEPPER, *Newsday*

ALL IT TAKES IS ALL YA GOT

Chris Gedney

Chris Gedney, 33, is a former tight end, with the Chicago Bears and Arizona Cardinals. He was a football standout at Syracuse University. He and his wife, Kathy, have two children and currently live in Cleveland, Ohio. Chris is an account executive for a mortgage company.

I couldn't make it to the services in California because of my job, but I was able to attend the private ceremonies at Sun Devil Stadium in Tempe, Arizona, on Friday night, May 7, 2004. It was pretty amazing. When I first got there, I'm looking around ASU Stadium, the athletic complex part of it, and I did see a lot of people I've not seen in a long time. I saw Jake Plummer, Dave McGinnis, Aaron Graham, and Larry Marmie, so there were a lot of hugs and handshakes. I remember walking out onto the field, and I wasn't ready for this part because I hadn't been back on the field in a while and, under the circumstances, it was a bit odd. Finally everyone took their seats, and I noticed the family was there, Marie, the two brothers and Pat's mom and dad. The family didn't speak at all and the mood was very somber.

Syracuse basketball coach Jim Boeheim was at one time also the head golf coach at Syracuse...Novelist, TV commentator, and former NFL defensive line star, Tim Green, was valedictorian of his senior class at Syracuse.

The program began with singing, and it was very moving. You got this feeling like you wanted to applaud for Pat—then I realized why I was there, so I didn't. The team chaplain for the Sun Devils,

You got this feeling like you wanted to applaud for Pat— then I realized why I was there...

whose name I can't remember but who played at ASU about ten years before Pat did, got up to speak and he really changed the mood. He asked everyone to do him a favor and give a round of applause for Pat. It was surreal, because five people stood and clapped, 10 more, then 20, and before we knew it, everyone was standing and clapping; it became a standing ovation. I think the message the chaplain was sending was we should be celebrating this great man. I'll tell you it helped to sort of break the ice for the rest of the night. There were beautiful flowers and banners of Pat Tillman and pictures in the different sections of the bleachers. It was amazing. The best part of the night was when everyone started to move around, and you got to see people you know, and you got to talk about things.

During the program, a young Asian lady approached the podium. I thought she would be reading some script, like one a university would put together that was sort of generic. She went on to talk about Pat Tillman—about the graduate work he was doing, about the special education course he'd taken and the people he'd befriended because of those classes, about the grade point average that he really did have, and about everything else Pat had done. The amazing thing is that all of this was sort of done under the radar; nobody knew, and it showed the academic side of Pat, which was truly amazing. The

> **The amazing thing is that all of this was sort of done under the radar; nobody knew...**

other part I liked was some people got up there and said, "Look, Pat wasn't exactly a saint." I believe his language is what kept him from sainthood. You could ask his college coach, Bruce Snyder, on that one. I guess Pat did have a wild-and-crazy side, too. I remember Cardinals training camp one year, where guys would be getting their ankles taped up at 7:20 in the morning. The eyes are wide awake but the rest of your body isn't at that time in the morning! Well, on this one morning, Pat was sitting there getting his ankles taped and he's got a 550-plus-page novel in his hand and he's reading it; he was just unusual!

Pat was the type who always wanted the opportunity to learn new things. During the 2000 season, I was just coming back from an illness, and Pat and I sat together on the trips back home after a game. We got along really well that year, and we had become close on road trips, flights or just killing time before or after a games or practices. We'd talk about things.

It's funny Pat never accepted all of the accolades; he would just shrug them off like they didn't mean anything to him. Pat Tillman didn't need a contract to play for the Cardinals; Pat Tillman did need a contract to do work for you—you talked about the terms, and you shook hands on it! I believe Pat was rare. I've heard that about his family if you had sealed a deal with them, they

> **It's funny Pat never accepted all of the accolades...**

would never waiver from that. That was a quality people liked in Pat.

In the 2000 season Pat had set the Cardinals' franchise record for total tackles in a season, and I won't tell you that I sat there and watched every single tackle, but I will tell you this: Something is wrong when you're the team's leading tackler and you're in the secondary; something is wrong, and our record reflected that. The defensive line and linebackers couldn't do the job, so Pat always picked up the slack by making tackles ten and fifteen yards down the field. Pat got the record that year, but he paid a price for it. Every time you would look at him coming off of the field you couldn't help but think, "Yeah! Torn sleeves. Blood. Grass stains." Yep, that was Pat!

Pat was a kickoff specialist in 2000 as well. Pat and our kicker, Cary Blanchard, kind of put their heads together and came up with a new onside kick. In a game, depending on what the call was from the sideline, Pat had the green light to use this new-found role and switch roles with Cary. Pat would run over and pooch-kick the football, as an onside kick. This happened at practice and in games. The neat thing was Pat hadn't done anything like that before, but he was a quick learner. That's the thing— if you needed someone, Pat was the guy. The answer was always, "Yes! I can do that," even if he hadn't done it before. I spoke to Dave McGinnis about that, and we both kind of broke down talking about it. That year, Vince Tobin had gotten fired about midway through the season, and we were 2-10 or something like that! We're playing Jacksonville at their place in the latter part of the year, and we all recall the play when Pat almost decapitated one of their receivers.

After the game, we were in the locker room, and we'd been blown out in the game. It was embarrassing. I remember in the locker room Pat giving out a speech. No, wait! It wasn't a speech. It was a good yelling! He said, "Do not give up! We can do better than this. If we can breathe, we can fight. And we can breathe,

"If we can breathe, we can fight. And we can breathe, so we can fight!"

so we can fight!" He echoed this six or seven more times at the top of his lungs not looking or pointing at any one person. I looked at his jersey, and he had blood stains, grass stains and pieces missing. At the time, the whole team was gathered around, and I was very close to where Pat was speaking. I'm almost thirty years old at the time, and here is a kid, not even the quarterback, standing before these men putting things into perspective. He was just simply out there playing as hard as he could. When he had knocked over a chair, he certainly had my attention.

The sad part about that was in later years, and even now, I'd come to realize that you have a choice—if you can breathe, you can fight. The sad part was that I saw certain guys roll their eyes, look at their watches, and make comments like, "Come on, man, we have a plane to catch." They missed the point. They missed why Pat was there and why he was doing it. When I asked Dave if he remembered, he said, "Absolutely, I remember the same thing." He replied that very few people got the message, that they missed it at the time. You should always give it all you've got. Sadly, there are so many people who just don't do that! Pat called it out, and it inspired me, even to this day.

I was getting ready to make a sales call in Florida, and I got the call from a good friend stating, "I don't know if you've heard or not, but Pat Tillman was killed in action sometime this morning or last night." I remember thinking and stating, "That can't be. Are you sure?" It was a real quick call. I ran into the office building where I had the meeting and just handed the gentlemen something and left. I almost got in three accidents in the five miles I

The first time I saw the dates was the hardest.

had to travel. I said, "That's it," and I just shut it down because I couldn't go on! I got back to the house and sure enough it's all over television, and, really, at that point, it all of a sudden became real for me. The first time I saw the dates was the hardest. I got my cell phone and started making calls. It was so hard. I thought about Rob Fredrickson, who was one of Pat's closest friends, who was asked to speak on Friday night, but he just couldn't. I think it would have been too hard on him.

Pat walked away from a lot and there has been a lot made about that, but Pat was well aware of the dangers that came with the duties of a U.S. Army Ranger. It would be very difficult for any of us to do that—to walk away from everything. It wasn't hard for Pat Tillman. I don't think he ever really looked at his decision with the extreme manner that ninety-five percent of the rest of our population did or would. He would have played for the Cardinals for free, just out of loyalty; that was who he was. I think Pat became bored with the NFL. I don't know if he would have played again because he didn't have the same emotion and energy. It seemed like after the attacks of 9/11, Pat wasn't the same person. His attention, emotions and energy were shifted. Like flipping a switch, he was driven now by something else. "If you can breathe, you can fight!" I now live my life by that phrase. It's my lasting memory of Pat and who he was, now that he's gone. I look forward to teaching my son about that because here is a guy who lived by what he said. Pat was everything you'd want your son to be.

> **Pat was well aware of the dangers that came with the duties of a U.S. Army Ranger.**

When I think of Pat Tillman, one word comes to mind: *unwavering*. If he set his mind to do something, he could do anything. He was unyielding. When I'd heard Pat on the radio announcing he was going to enlist in the Rangers, I tried to call him right away. I knew that once he made that announcement, he would follow it through all the way. Last year, Pat got to spend about six hours with Coach McGinnis and Larry Marmie during a game with Seattle, and they went to breakfast that morning. After Pat left, Coach made the comment that he felt bad because he didn't even care about a win or a loss—all he could remember was his time he'd spent with Pat Tillman. Pat was that special!

Pat wasn't a very spiritual person, however; he always would listen to what I talked about with him in regards to my faith as a Christian, but we never really went deep into those matters. Pat was highly educated. I know he knew about Christianity and other religions—he knew the facts. I don't know where he was in those final minutes on the battlefield, but I like to believe Pat had made a choice.

God bless Pat Tillman!

E PLURIBUS UNUM

Larry Marmie

Marmie was Tillman's defensive coordinator with the Arizona Cardinals and was in constant contact with Tillman after he joined the Rangers. The two became friends, and Marmie was asked to speak at both of Tillman's memorial services.

He had a charisma about him. The secretaries liked him. The custodians liked him. Little kids gravitated to him. In my heart, I thought there is no way this could happen. It just couldn't be that kind of story.

Pat died fighting for what he believed in. His courage and convictions are what this country is built on. He is a hero to us all.

A lot of people knew Pat Tillman because he was a football player. The real sad part is that they didn't know Pat Tillman as a person. What we lost in terms of a person is really something that a lot of us would like to have... those kinds of convictions and the kind of character and attitude that he had about living life. He was highly intelligent, and very committed to being good at what he did, not just football, but whatever he did. He just had a charisma about him and everyone just gravitated to him.

In my mind, Pat Tillman was the guy we all wanted to be like. Pat lived life on his terms. He walked away from the comfort and the material things most of us desire. He sought out danger for what he deemed to be a greater good. Pat was true to his heart—a worthy role model! Here's somebody who embodied the very concept of 'role model.'

He had a strong dislike for the easy way out. He was caring. He was thoughtful. He was soft—Pat was soft… in the heart. He was humble yet confident, reserved but he was hard. You wanted this guy on your team and it didn't have to be a football team. You wanted him on your team in anything you were doing.

Some people wondered why Pat did what he did. There had to be some other reason, other than he felt it was the right thing to do. But simply put, that *was* his motivation.

One of my favorite memories of Pat was in the summer in Tempe, Arizona, when it was 100 to 120 degrees. Usually when we got done with our mini-camp work, (Cardinals coach) Dave McGinnis and I would run on this jogging trail on Warner Road. So many of those days, we'd be somewhere into our run, and here came Pat down Warner Road, windows down in his jeep—he didn't have air conditioning—he didn't want it. Windows down, long hair flying, he'd stick his head out the window and say, "Pick it up, coach, pick it up. Faster. Pick the pace up."

It was fun coaching Pat. It was challenging coaching Pat. It was an honor to coach Pat.

I learned a lot from him. Players are usually trying to earn the respect of their coach. I found myself trying to earn Pat's respect.

This community embraced Pat because of what he was as a player, and he became even more of a favorite once they started to find out what kind of person he was. Pat's values were not distorted by natural things. He wasn't about glamour and glitz. He was true to his heart. He believed in looking forward, not backward. He was all about the truth. And he didn't care about trying to impress some un-appointed judge. Pat was not motivated by a fear of failure. He was motivated by his pursuit of excellence. In my mind Pat's life had one primary objective—be the best you can be in whatever endeavor you undertake.

Don't worry about the score. Don't worry about the image. Don't worry about the opponent. It sounds real easy, but actually it is very difficult.

As time passes, I believe we will all learn to appreciate even more what Pat Tillman has taught us. Pat was really a simple guy, wanted to be one of the boys. But he understood life, and he pursued excellence and understanding. Someone once said a person who knows how will always have a job, and a person who knows why will be his boss. Pat understood both. To me it seemed like he was always playing chess and I was playing checkers.

Pat did not believe in taking the path of least resistance, which a lot of us like to look for. In my mind he was a person we would all like to be.

I'll never ever see another No. 40 that doesn't bring Pat to mind every time I see that number.

SOME INJURED PLAYERS ARE LISTED "DAY-TO-DAY" … BUT WE'RE ALL DAY-TO-DAY

John Omohundro

John has been a trainer with the Cardinals for 38 years, the last 34 as the team's head trainer.

Pat had a way of making trainers look good, because he was so tough. At the same time Pat was very set in his ways in what he wanted to do and how he wanted to do it. There was a time he had a very severe ankle sprain in Philadelphia, and he refused to be carted off. His mindset was he could do whatever he wanted. It was a real challenge for us. Everything we would do might not be as much as he thought should be done. He'd want to do more and the ankle would stay swollen. Rest was not in his vocabulary. He was one hundred percent work.

He was a very dedicated type of guy. Some guys would be on the treatment table, they'd be reading out of a prayer book. Pat would be off in some distant novel, some book that caught his interest or fancy. He was just a unique individual. You don't meet many of those people in a lifetime.

Our nickname for him the first couple of years was Spiccoli, from the movie *Fast Times at Ridgemont High*.

He looked like Sean Penn—party on, dude. That just seemed like that was Pat, but as you got to know him a little bit more, you realized he was no dummy. He was the real deal, very intelligent. He was on a different plane than most of the guys.

I can remember standing up there at Flagstaff one year, it was the first couple of practices and Mac, Coach Dave McGinnis, said we were going to go about half speed, but Pat was going full speed. He didn't know how to tone it down. When he stepped on the field, he was balls-out. That's the only way he knew.

When I first saw him I wondered how he played linebacker. He was small, even as a defensive back. I really didn't know how to take him. I knew he was always around the ball, a very active type guy, at ASU. When we called about players' injuries before the draft, we talked to Perry, then ASU trainer, Perry Edinger. He said, "Man, you get him. He's something. You don't have to worry about anything he's got because he'll play with it."

My son was at a restaurant one night. Pat came over to him, sat down and talked to him for a while. People came up and said, "Hey aren't you Pat Tillman?" He said, "No. No. I get confused for being Pat Tillman all the time." He said, "I work for Tempe sanitation detail. My route is down there on Baseline and 48th Street." They said, "You look like Pat Tillman." He said, "No. No." My son, Jim, was absolutely ready to break up; he put on such a convincing story.

The only real injury the guy had when he was here was that ankle. We said, "Pat, hold on out there on the field. Just be patient with us. We're going to get the cart out there. He looked at me, and said, "I'm not taking any cart off the field." He was bound and determined. He said, "You bring that cart out here and the guy is going to ride it back by himself."

When we got back to Arizona, he refused to use crutches, and he refused to wear one of those boots to immobilize it. On Wednesday, when we went out to practice, Pat came in and got taped up. We said, "Pat, you can't practice on that. Pat said, "Tape me up. I'm supposed to be out on the field." He started walking around on the other field from where the team was practicing, and he said, "I know I can't practice, but I'm going to get this thing well." We said, "You're supposed to be on crutches." He said, "No, no." He'd walk around and say, "This isn't getting any ——— better." He'd ask for another tape job. He asked for everything. He just had to be convinced he had a bad ankle.

He'd always feel like the injury was letting the team down and his teammates down. It was one of those devastating high-ankle sprains that take people eight weeks to come back from. He played at the end of five, and he thought that was just awful.

He was a very low-maintenance guy. He had a wrist injury, and he refused diagnostics on for fear it'd be something worse than it was. We told him we'd give him a cast. He said, "I'm not wearing a ——— cast." He didn't come in here unless he really, really had to.

I really felt like he took a lot of that stuff on himself personally about our lack of success. He really felt if there was a strong enough will, by enough people they could overcome this losing attitude. He had willed himself into those positions at every level. "Pat you're too small to play football. Pat, you're not enough of this—you're not enough of that." He *was* too small to play linebacker, and he *was* the Pac-10 defensive player of the year. He was a projection at safety in the NFL, because he had never played there, yet he came out and excelled at it.

When we saw each other in Seattle last year, we just talked. I said, "This is going to be an event worth getting out of the deathbed for when they see you running out of that tunnel at Sun Devil Stadium." He just said, "Thanks, I'm looking forward to it."

Even our heroes are not immune from the clutches of death in between the despicable and the innocent must stand mighty men—and women—of valor.

Pat Tillman was one of those valiant people. And though he's gone in physical form, you may rest assured that we are still safe. There are others who will take his place and fill the gap, men and women that will also lay down their lives for you and I, if they are so required.
—MIKE ROSIER, *The* (S. C.) *Times and Democrat*

Pat had a wonderful sense of humor. The person who thought he was the funniest was Pat—he thought he was hysterical. And he was. He loved his friends and his family 'cause we laughed at his jokes. He had an infectious and booming laugh. His head would roll back and his hands would go wide, and his eyes would get all slanty. He would do that laugh anytime, anywhere and damn the consequences. If he was in a restaurant, and people were disturbed, he was looking at them, going, "I don't know why you're not laughing 'cause this is really funny." And his laugh came really often.

You just couldn't help but laugh when you were with him. You just couldn't help but laugh at him. He had this Christmas sweater and pink slippers and a kimono, which he thought were cool. He often talked about how blond his hair was. When it was cool to have it long, he had it short. When it was cool to have it short, he had it long. He was proud of his mono-brow. He thought there was a conspiracy by all those folks who were tall against people like him who were short.

He had a wonderful sense of self-deprecation. Pat and my friend, Todd, are godfathers for my son, Adam. There's no godmothers so Pat decided to come to the baptism *dressed as the godmother*, dressed as a woman. He changed, but that's Pat—making fun of himself. When my son, Ryan, was born, Pat was in Arizona at a minicamp. We certainly didn't expect to see him so we're in the room holding little Ryan and doing our thing. All of a sudden, out in the hall, you just hear this, "Every day's Sunday, baby!" He kicks open the door, bursts in, absolutely scares the living hell out of Ryan, wakes up all the other kids on the floor—but that was Pat. Coming home, being funny, but showing his commitment to his family. It was priceless.

—ALEX GARWOOD, Pat Tillman's brother-in-law

Chapter 4

The Write Stuff

A Tillman Reader
For Tillman Readers

Since 9/11, all Arizona Cardinals strong safety Pat Tillman wanted was to fight for his country. He took a potential $1,182,000 annual pay cut to jump from the NFL to the Army Rangers in 2002, and he refused all attempts to glorify his decision. He told friends that he wanted to be treated as no more special than the guy on the cot next to him. ("He viewed his decision as no more patriotic than that of his less fortunate, less renowned countrymen," Arizona senator John McCain said.) Tillman even forbade his family and friends from talking to the press about him. News crews begged for photos, mere shots of him signing his induction papers or piling out of a truck at Fort Benning, Ga., or getting his first haircut—anything. They got nothing.

Tillman died a hero and a patriot. But his death is a wake-up call to the nation that every day—more than 500 times since President Bush declared "Major combat operations in Iraq have ended," more than 800 times since the invasion of Afghanistan—a family must drive to the airport to greet their dead child. The only difference this time is that the whole country knew this child.

Athletes are soldiers and soldiers are athletes. Uniformed, fit and trained, they fight for one cause, one team. They take ground and they defend it. Both are carried off on their teammates' shoulders, athletes when they win and soldiers when they die.

—**RICK REILLY**, *Sports Illustrated*

A tribesman rode with them, a Taliban sympathizer. He was a plant who had offered to take the Rangers to a hidden enemy arms dump. Instead he was leading them into a trap. That's what Taliban sources would report later, after the air ripped just outside of Spera at half past seven and everything went to hell.

The Rangers scrambled out of their vehicles as they came under ambush and charged the militants on foot.

Suddenly Pat was down, Pat was dying. Two other U.S. soldiers were wounded, and a coalition Afghani fighter was killed in the fire-fight that lasted 15 or 20 minutes before the jihadists melted away. That's what the American military says.

Pat's truck hit a land mine, and he died from wounds caused by the explosion. That's what an Afghani coalition commander says. Either way, on Monday, four days later, Kevin made the long flight home with his brother's body.

The news whistled through America's soul and raised the hair on the back of its neck. It tapped into people's admiration, their awe, their guilt. In a country where no civilians have been asked to sacrifice anything and where even the cost of the war is being forwarded to their children and their children's children, a man had sacrificed the biggest dream of all. The NFL.

During World War II, 638 NFL players served and 19 died in action, but no well-known U.S. professional athletes in a quarter century had volunteered for service, and none had perished since Buffalo Bill lineman Bob Kalsu in Vietnam in 1970.

Memorials sprang up overnight, balloons and flowers and teddy bears and notes left, and a man stood before a photo of Pat outside Sun Devil Stadium—home to ASU and the Cardinals—and blew *Amazing Grace* through his bagpipes. Scholarships were founded, and the Cardinals announced that a plaza outside their unfinished new stadium will carry his name. Before its story had even been written, SI had received 103 letters about Pat's sacrifice. Pat had no need for the fuss. But the people did. At last they had a face to grieve.

—*GARY SMITH*, Sports Illustrated

It would be perfectly fitting to name a stadium or parkway or mountain after Pat Tillman. But it's not really necessary. His life story is so compelling and so well known that for the rest of your life you will read of extraordinary acts by courageous people who describe Tillman as their inspiration. That will be his mountain. And it won't stop growing.

—**PHIL BOAS**, deputy editorial page editor,
The Arizona Republic

"What I must do is all that concerns me, not what the people think… you will always find those who think they know what is your duty better than you know it. It is easy in the world to live after the world's opinion; it is easy in the solitude to live after our own; but the great man is he who in the midst of the crowd keeps with perfect sweetness the independence of solitude."

—**RALPH WALDO EMERSON**, Poet, Inscription on memorial
card at San Jose Pat Tillman Memorial service

PAT TILLMAN? THUMBS UP!

Richard Roeper, *Chicago Sun-Times*

Even at 8 a.m. on a Friday, there are a few clusters of gamblers huddled around the blackjack and craps tables.

You get the *Las Vegas Review-Journal* and the *Los Angeles Times*, and you buy your big coffee, and you get on the elevator with a couple of guys in Boston Red Sox caps. They're still grousing about their blackjack luck from the night before.

"I didn't get one blackjack all night," one says. "It was wicked ret-ah-ded."

In the hallway, you pass a maid who greets you with a sunny smile and says, "Make sure you get outside and enjoy this beautiful day."

> **It takes you a minute to absorb the news— Tillman, Tillman...**

You're planning to do just that but for now you have to absorb the news of the day, so settle in with the papers and turn on the TV in your room.

Some jock is meeting with the press. He's saying something about playing with somebody for a year and being grateful for the opportunity to know him. That's not what players say when a teammate has been traded or retires. You focus on the screen, and the news crawl spells it out: "PAT TILLMAN, 1976-2004."

It takes you a minute to absorb the news—Tillman, Tillman...That's right. The young man who gave up the football career to serve his country. Like most other sports fans, you were mightily impressed when you first heard that Tillman was going to put his NFL career on hold to join the Army. And then, like most sports fans, you forgot about Pat Tillman.

Not that Tillman would have cared. His crusade had nothing to do with winning our applause and attention. In fact, he consistently ducked the media spotlight after he joined the Army.

The stories about Tillman invariably mentioned that he had given up a $3.6 million deal with the Arizona Cardinals to fight for his country for a paycheck of about $1,500 a month. As if the real sacrifice were about money. As if that were more important than saying goodbye to one's wife, one's family and friends, in order to fight in a battle that held only passing interest to many Americans.

Your guess is that if Tillman could have written the lead for his own obituary, it wouldn't even mention the money or his football career. He'd probably want it to go something like this:

> "Since the Fall of 2001, more than 100 American soldiers have been killed in the line of duty in Afghanistan, and more than 700 have been killed in Iraq. Their ranks include Pat Tillman, a proud member of the Army Rangers."

The only drafts we have nowadays involve sports teams selecting gifted young athletes—and one day after we learned of Tillman's death, the NFL started conducting its annual draft.

When Eli Manning was announced as the No. 1 overall pick, he was crestfallen. Wrong team! Manning and family sulked for an hour, and he talked about sitting out for a year. If he had to play for the San Diego Chargers, he'd rather not play at all. Then Manning was traded to the team of his choice, and he beamed for the cameras.

It was an obscenely selfish and childish spectacle. Even as NFL Commissioner Paul Tagliabue wore a black ribbon and a Cardinals pin to honor Tillman, even as fans broke into chants of "U-S-A! U-S-A!", Manning played the part of the me-first superstar. All the talk about Tillman's death "putting things into perspective" and "reminding us who the real heroes are" didn't penetrate Manning's psyche for one thin second.

You're here in Vegas for an annual reunion with about 30 friends. The laughs keep coming, all weekend long. On Saturday, the Red Sox fans go wild when their guys beat the New York Yankees. On the big-screen TVs in the sports book, you get lots of replays. There's Eli Manning grimacing when the Chargers select him.

His whole life is ahead of him.

There's Pat Tillman celebrating big plays on the football field.

His whole life is behind him.

NOT EVEN SAMSON CAN TEAR DOWN HIS COLUMNS

Scott Bordow

Scott Bordow, 43, is the sports columnist for the East Valley Tribune, *a suburban paper outside Phoenix. He covered Tillman at Arizona State and with the Arizona Cardinals.*

It's so hard to know where to begin describing Pat, but one story keeps leaping out at me. I remember interviewing him when he was a sophomore at ASU. He had the long hair back then and called everybody "dude." People didn't know what to make of him. He told me that he wanted to make one million dollars by the time he was thirty years old…and he *didn't* want it to come from football.

Pat was just different. He had his 2000 look about him but 1950s sensibilities. His whole life was a paradox. You'd look at him and think he belonged on MTV, but he was one of the most respectful people I've met. He didn't brush off people like a lot of athletes. It didn't matter if you were an equipment manager or the president of the university, he cared about what you had to say.

Pat liked to swear. Everybody knew that. But it was such a part of him that it didn't seem like it was a big deal. And it wasn't meant disrespectfully or for shock value. It was just the way he talked.

One of the stories I love about Pat is that on the rare occasions the defensive coaches took him out of the game, he'd yell "touchdown," as he went to the sideline. It was his not-so-subtle way of telling the coaches that if he wasn't in, the other team was going to score.

It was amazing watching Pat play. He wasn't the biggest or fastest athlete on the field, but he was always coming up with the big plays. Some of it was because he was so smart. He studied film while other players slept through the meetings. In fact, if a player incorrectly answered a question in the meeting, Pat would yell, "Wrong!" Nobody got mad at him. That was Pat.

Like everybody else, I tried to get Pat to do an interview after he became a Ranger. I asked a mutual friend to ask Pat if he'd be willing to sit down for an interview. The friend told me that Pat said, "Dude, tell Scott I like him, but I'm not talking." It didn't surprise me. Once Pat put his mind to something, that was it.

A lot of people said Pat enlisted because of September 11. That was certainly the impetus, but I believe he had become bored with football at that point. It couldn't satisfy the appetite for life he had. When 9/11 occurred, and his brother Kevin said he was going to sign up, Pat felt it was the right thing to do by his brother and the right thing to do by his country.

I covered his memorial service at San Jose and the one Arizona State had at Sun Devil Stadium. It's incredible how many people he touched. I talked to a Vietnam War veteran in San Jose who said that every week his local chapter goes to the cemetery and reads off the names of fellow chapter members who served in Vietnam and died. He said they were going to read Pat Tillman's name that following Saturday.

One of the things I appreciated about Pat was his honesty. So many athletes revert to *clichés* when talking about their sport or the game they just played. Pat was always honest. If his team stunk, he'd say it. He was what reporters called a go-to guy.

I've heard hundreds of stories about Pat since he died. I'll add one of my own. I remember asking him when he was going to marry Marie, his high school sweetheart. This was late in his career at ASU. "I don't know, dude," he'd say. At that point, he was a star, and women were throwing themselves at him. I asked him if it was difficult to stay faithful to Marie. He looked at me like I was nuts. "Dude, she's my girl," he said, and that was that.

I've met thousands of athletes in my twenty years in journalism. Pat wasn't like the rest of them.

I am a sailor serving in Kuwait, in support of Operation Iraqi Feedom II. I am attached to Naval Supply Support Battalion 1, out of the reserve center at 35th Avenue.

My shipmates and I would like to express our sympathy to the family of Pat Tillman. His story has been inspiring and well-followed by many of us ever since he enlisted. He chose to serve and exhibited the honor and bravery that makes the stuff of legends.

His parents should be proud that their son left such a mark on this world and nation, and they should be proud of raising a hero.

—BRIAN C. IRIZARRY, Mesa, AZ

TOO GOOD TO BE TRUE

Doug MacEachern, Columnist, *The Arizona Republic*

I do not know the family of Pat Tillman, so I cannot grieve with them. I can offer my condolences, sincere and heavy as a millstone. But you do not grieve with strangers.

I do not know his friends or the athletes with whom he played football or the soldiers with whom he served. Since the first reports of the soldier's death in Afghanistan, I have heard them on radio and watched them on TV expressing their awful pain. But, again, they don't know or need me. They need each other.

The anguish of the reporters who knew Pat Tillman is crushing.

But I can grieve with reporters. The veneer of stoic, set-apart indifference—usually feigned, of course—that so annoys people who are not reporters is nowhere to be found.

The anguish of the reporters who knew Pat Tillman is crushing. You can feel it in what they write.

I have never envied sports reporters. The travel is a burden; the hours are lousy. Where others go for fun, they go for work. But the worst of it, I always thought, was that their jobs required them to endure self-absorbed modern-day athletes, whose astonishing capacity to whine, complain and generate misery among those around them all but overwhelms the stories of accomplishment on the fields.

Political reporters may have to suffer the egos of elected officials, but at least the pols tend to come tamped down a bit with the mellowing influence of age. There is nothing quite so brimming with an unbridled sense of entitlement as a locker room full of excessively pampered, insanely over-paid, young men.

Then, there was Tillman.

As I noted, I never knew the man. Only some of the people who wrote about him. And I have never known an athlete to have the kind of effect on reporters that Tillman had on them.

There are athletes whom reporters respect, of course. There are plenty who are entertaining and fun to be around. And there are others who seem capable enough outside the realm of sports that it is apparent to those writing about them that they aren't likely to squander their fortunes.

But almost no pro athletes ever just walk away from the money, and certainly none of them in modern times ever walked away from their sports world millions to serve in the military.

That alone would mark Tillman as an extraordinary human being. But the reason he so inspired even hardened reporters wasn't just because he announced one day he would join the Army Rangers with his brother, forgoing a million-dollar contract extension with the Arizona Cardinals. Pat Tillman was inspiring because his announcement was unsurprising to those who knew him.

Looking back through the clip files from May 2002, when Tillman decided to leave the NFL for the Army, I could find no story in which Tillman produced some syrupy, sentimentalized explanation for his decision. His motivations were plain enough: He joined up seven months after the Sept. 11, 2001 attacks. He felt a sense of duty, of obligation—qualities so rare that it was difficult for many people at the time to fully grasp that they were in fact his real reasons. Surely, this bold act must be part of some grander plan. Like a run for office?

> **I could find no story in which Tillman produced some syrupy, sentimentalized explanation for his decision.**

Perhaps the most endearing aspect of Tillman's decision among reporters—you could see it oozing from their clips—was that he went into the service quietly, with no "farewell" statement at all. No bravado and no apparent wish to be seen as the hero he inevitably became. The modesty alone is breathtaking. Where do they, indeed, find people such as this?

"He viewed his decision as no more patriotic than that of his less fortunate, less renowned countrymen who loved our country enough to volunteer to defend her in a time of peril," U.S. Sen. John McCain said.

And, indeed, Tillman is but one of 110 U.S. soldiers killed in Afghanistan since the war there began—39 of them killed, as Tillman was, in combat.

The loss of each of those soldiers is a searing pain to someone, of course. Tillman's loss is not extraordinary in that respect.

Which no doubt is how he would want to be remembered. As one, unassuming, among many.

HE LIVES IN THE QUAD CITIES— TWICE AS NICE AS THE TWIN CITIES

Bill Wundram

Bill Wundram is the Sage of Davenport, Iowa and was known as "The Enforcer" in his heyday of suiting up for the Quad-City Thunder CBA team. He compares Pat Tillman to Heisman legend Nile Kinnick.

B ack in 1943, Bill Cunningham of the Boston Globe wrote: "As long as America has the Nile Kinnicks of the world to protect her, we will be OK." It was written at the time of Kinnick's tragic wartime death.

Now, in 2004, as long as America has the Pat Tillmans of the world to protect her; we will be OK.

There are parallels between Iowa's **Nile Kinnick**, 24, and Arizona's Pat Tillman, 27.

Both died for their country.

Tillman gave up a $3.6 million pro football contract with the Arizona Cardinals to enlist in the service and become an Army Ranger. He was killed in Afghanistan, a fire fight.

Kinnick gave up a lucrative professional football career with the NFL's Brooklyn Dodgers. Before Pearl Harbor, he enlisted in the Navy. He was a fighter pilot aboard the

Nile Kinnick is the only Heisman Trophy winner to have a stadium named after him. The Iowa Hawkeyes play in Nile Kinnick Stadium.

aircraft carrier Lexington and died in '43 when the motor of his plane failed and crashed into the sea.

There are other comparisons between the two athletes.

Both were football players of exceptional ability.

Both were undersized athletes in a game of big guys. Kinnick was 5-9 and 170 pounds. Tillman, at 5-11, weighed 199 pounds.

Both were articulate, intelligent. Kinnick, a Phi Beta Kappa, graduated with a 3.40 grade average. Tillman graduated summa cum laude in 3½ years from Arizona State University with a 3.84 grade average.

The University of Iowa football field, as everyone should know, is named for Nile Kinnick.

In Phoenix, the plaza surrounding the new Cardinals stadium, will be named Pat Tillman Freedom Plaza.

We're reminded of the legacy of Kinnick at the start of every Big 10 football game. The coin that is tossed bears Kinnick's likeness. Since Coach Kirk Ferentz took over, Iowa has won a statistically remarkable number of tosses. It can be said that Nile still helps the team whenever he can.

When Kinnick won the Heisman Trophy in 1939, he said, famously: "I thank God I was warring on the gridirons of the Midwest and not on the battlefields of Europe. I can speak confidently and positively that the players of this country would much rather struggle and fight to win the Heisman Award than the Croix de Guerre."

The Associated Press wrote the next day:

"The kid from the corn country took it in stride and when he finished his classic speech, and 700 men and women rose and cheered and whistled, you tried to gulp down a lump in your throat. You realized the ovation wasn't alone for Nile Kinnick, the outstanding football player of the year. It was also for **Nile Kinnick**, typifying everything admired in American youth."

It wasn't until Nile's dad died that the Iowa stadium was renamed for Kinnick. His father had long opposed the move, saying that Nile was too modest for such an honor.

Kinnick's fame spread around the world. There is a Nile C. Kinnick High School in Yokohama, Japan. A huge stadium was built in Tokyo for the 1940 Olympics. The

It wasn't until Nile's dad died that the Iowa stadium was renamed for Kinnick.

stadium survived bombing during World War II, and upon arrival of American occupation forces, it was named Nile C. Kinnick Stadium. There is a question if that name still stands.

The end, finis for the tale of two heroes. Kinnick's name is obscure to many today. Tillman's name is fresh in our minds. Yet, there stands remarkable analogies to these gridiron greats, both in life and in death. They were brave hearts, far beyond the cheer of gridiron crowds....

Nile Kinnick was a catcher in American Junior Legion baseball in Adel, Iowa. His pitcher was Bob Feller, later to make baseball's Hall of Fame.

PICTURE THIS

Tim Tyers

Tim has been a sportswriter for Phoenix Newspapers, Inc., for almost 35 years. He began in 1966, and was an ASU beat writer for many years for The Phoenix Gazette. *He has always been one to get to know both coaches and players, and while he did not personally cover Pat, he followed the program closely as an Arizona Republic columnist.*

I was doing a story on Pat's triathlon. We had to set up a picture. I had it all set up for three o'clock, and Pat and his buddy came by. We wanted a shot on the bicycle. This is well after practice, but he takes the time to come back to where we were. The photographer had to cancel the photo for that time and told us to ask Pat if he could come back at five o'clock. I just knew we weren't going to be able to get the picture. I went in to Pat and said, "Hey, Pat, there's been a foul-up. The photographer had to go somewhere else right now, and they want to know if you'd be willing to shoot it at five o'clock." He says, "Hey, dude, no problem. I'll be back." And he did—on his own. He went home and he came back. And, we shot the picture. He was doing all this for charity and was selling the miles and everything—all of it went to some children's charity. You don't find that a hell of a lot among athletes.

You would try to interview him sometimes, and it was just like talking to a stone wall.

When Pat got a concussion in Denver, he sneaked back into the game. Coach McGinnis finally had to say, "The next guy that lets him have a helmet is gone." He got Pat's helmet and took it back to the locker room, and Pat borrowed another guy's helmet and went back in the game. That's what made McGinnis so mad.

When Pat was in high school, his team was up by about fifty points so the coach took everybody out. Pat put himself back in and ran a punt back for a score. One of his high school coaches heard that Pat was in trouble, so he went around to where he was and said, "Pat, what were you doing up on the roof?" Well, he had been bombing people with water balloons.

His principal once said to me, "Pat was an individual, but he traveled in packs the size of **soccer** teams."

> More U.S. kids play soccer today than any organized sport, including youth football. The reason so many kids play soccer is so they don't have to watch it.

Tillman's death is such a shame. But let's not forget the hundreds of other soldiers who have died in this conflict. Famous or not, in the eyes of their children, parents and spouses, these lesser-known soldiers were the world.

Let us mourn them all. And let us always remember Pat Tillman, a truly amazing American.

—**PETE BARTH**, *The Sheboygan* (Wis.) *Press*

ONE MAN, ONE SACRIFICE

Marianne Jennings

Marianne Jennings is a professor of legal and ethical studies in business at Arizona State University. In addition, her weekly columns are syndicated around the country, and her work has appeared in the Wall Street Journal, *the* Chicago Tribune, *the* New York Times, *and the* Washington Post.

I swung by the Pat Tillman makeshift memorial near Sun Devil Stadium on my campus. The hats, footballs, balloons and hastily crafted signed flapped eerily on an unusually windy day. A passerby drew me into conversation: "It's quite a tribute."

Blinded by the Mylar balloons, I didn't quite see it that way. If it hadn't been for the redeeming colonial "Don't tread on me" flag wrapped around a Saguaro cactus, I would have flung the deposited trinkets into the wind as if they were moneychangers in the temple.

Why does everybody famous get the same treatment upon tragic passing: Care Bears and poster board signs courtesy of Sharpie pens? How dare they treat this man in the same fashion as they did Princess Diana and Versace! Mr. Tillman was head and shoulders above those jet setters and shallow mavens of design.

This soul of indomitable courage left us, but our memorial is no different from those impromptu ones created for the likes of Kurt Cobain. The media hoopla is the same, for fame is fame, and it sells, regardless of its origins.

Worse, the Tillman media coverage minimizes the sacrifice of all those who have given their lives for freedom. Their lack of a pro football career lessens their nobility in this era of reality TV and surreal life. Every man's death diminishes us, but we slight the locals to worship and mourn the famous and infamous.

This business of sobbing for the famous we have never met, from druggies to playboys, has troubled me for a decade. Fans just held a 10-year memorial service for druggie Cobain. Rapper Tupac Shakur's death got more media coverage than Mother Teresa's. We mark the anniversary of Princess Diana's death. We have candlelight vigils on the anniversary of Elvis' overdose.

> **This pedestal treatment would be an affront to Mr. Tillman.**

I blame Don McLean. He lionized Buddy Holly with his tribute, "The Day The Music Died." The music world progressed nicely even after Mozart's passing, but it can't continue because the man who wrote the "Peggy Sue" songs died in a plane crash?

With Mr. Tillman's passing, we fall into a trap of placing courage exercised by the rich and famous as more of an 18-year-old on the same battlefront who was there with the same burning desire for freedom. All he left behind was a Jeep with bald tires, so, we discount his ultimate sacrifice.

This pedestal treatment would be an affront to Mr. Tillman. All men are created equal, especially in death.

But, the famous are our family and friends. We mourn vicariously for those we never met.

We miss and dismiss the valor and deeds of the common man. Have the copyright restrictions limiting its air-play taken hold so strongly that no one remembers the moral of "It's A Wonderful Life?" Lives lived the right way, and not necessarily in the spotlight, matter.

We prefer our first-name closeness with the shallow icons of our day. I was in a waiting room this past week when CNN announced that Michael Jackson had fired his legal team and hired fresh bottom-feeders for trial. Two women who shared the waiting room and wait with me, one in gold sandals and Sarasota leather skin, gasped and chatted in great detail about this strategically foolish move.

"Mark is just too busy with the Laci trial," she exclaimed. But, her friend, wearing a portrait of a FTD shop on her blouse, disagreed, "Yes, but Mark's a likeable lawyer, and Michael needs that."

The conversation smacked of two pontificating great aunts from Long Island, whose advice and experience are often ignored because of their sartorial lapses. These two women, miles from Santa Maria, Calif., and Neverland, opined as if Michael were their nephew and Mark Geragos, the fired Jackson lawyer, was a neighbor.

Society's deepest feelings are for the famous who enter their homes via cable and satellite. It took me almost one year to understand that when people said that they voted for Ruben that they were not discussing a national Subway sandwich contest, but rather, American Idol. They were talking about a television show that turns ordinary folks into famous folks, some for their talent, and others for the lack thereof.

They are all equal in the eyes of a nation enamored of fame. Idol worship. Could Moses have been a network visionary?

> **Mr. Tillman resisted media coverage because he understood that fame is irrelevant.**

Which brings me to Barbara Walters and the on-camera adoption of a child. Walters has allowed a teen mother to use national, prime-time TV to auction off a child to five desperate couples. *People* magazine, Oprah, et al. will note mom's courage and cover her life and the child's. Dignity, where art thou?

The era when out-of-wedlock mothers had the decency to be discreet and lived out trimesters two and three with aunts in Long Island looks good.

Mr. Tillman's life and lessons are many, but we're missing the most important: Discretion is the greater part of valor. Mr. Tillman resisted media coverage because he understood that fame is irrelevant. His sacrifice was a testament to his belief that principled lives, not pro sports contracts, matter.

Sacrifices for freedom are created equal. All of our brave soldiers, from Long Island to Sarasota, from 18-year-old dropout to college graduate linebacker, are equal. Mourn accordingly, and use some discretion on the passing of the infamous.

Pat Tillman climbing his favorite light tower at Sun Devil Stadium

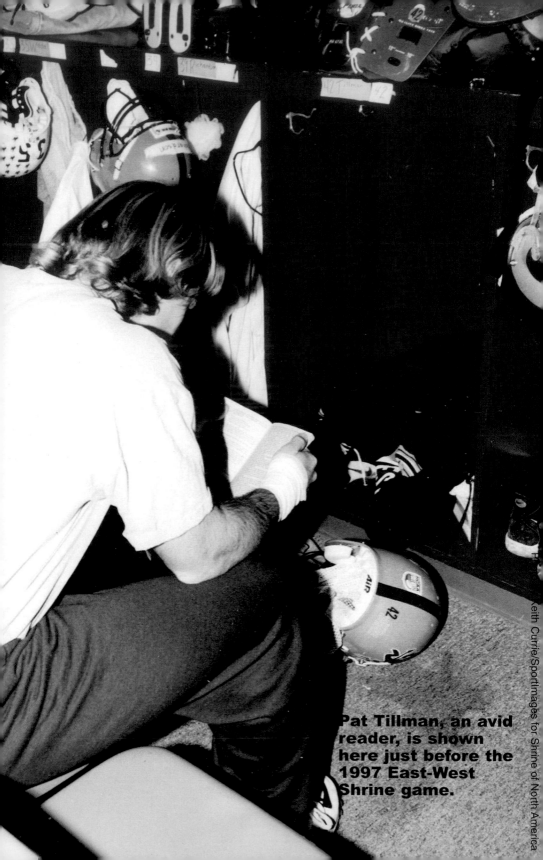

Pat Tillman, an avid reader, is shown here just before the 1997 East-West Shrine game.

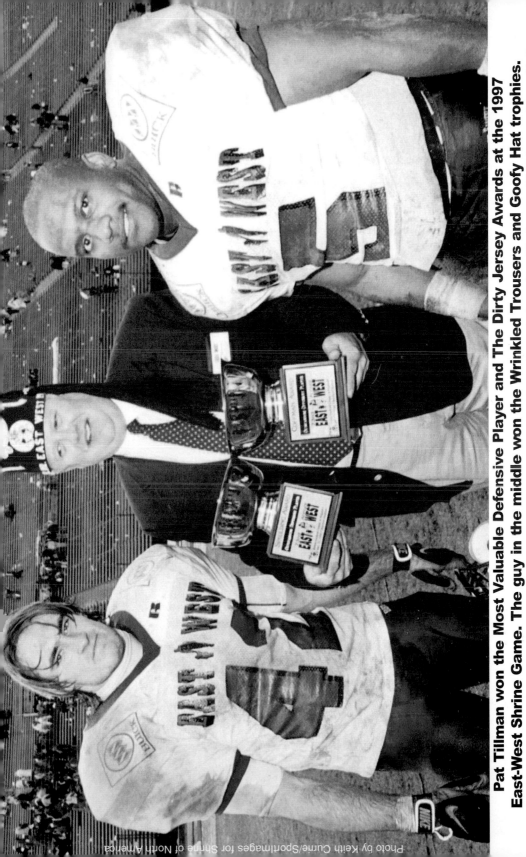

Pat Tillman won the Most Valuable Defensive Player and The Dirty Jersey Awards at the 1997 East-West Shrine Game. The guy in the middle won the Wrinkled Trousers and Goofy Hat trophies. Actually, his name is Bob Menary, who has worked countless hours for the Shriners Childrens Hospitals.

Stanford coach Tyrone Willingham giving instructions to the West Team at the annual Shrine Game in 1997

Pat Tillman arrives at Cardinals training camp on his Beemer Escalade bicycle

Donovan McNabb, meet Mr. Tillman

"I could be...QB."

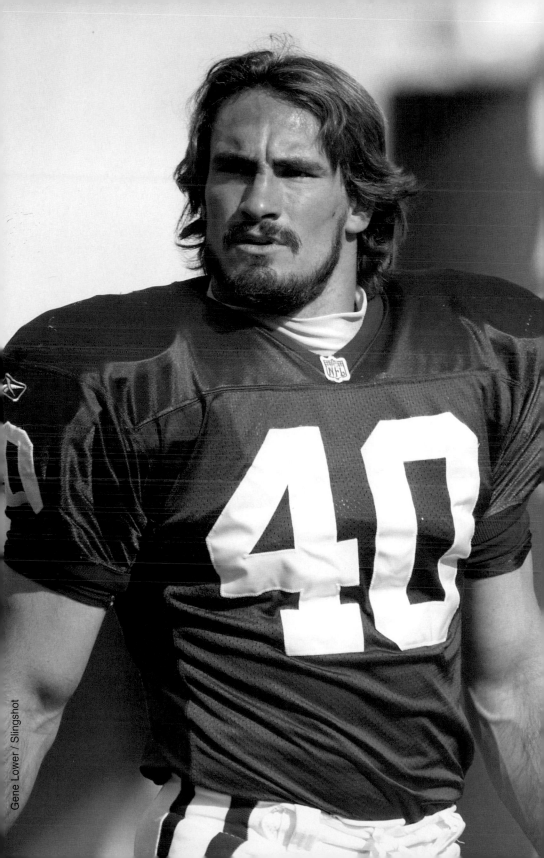

Pat Tillman leaving the football field for the last time

Gene Lower / Slingshot

Sports Illustrated

AN ATHLETE DIES A SOLDIER
PAT TILLMAN
1976 – 2004

MAY 3, 2004 www.si.com
AOL Keyword: Sports Illustrated

PAT TILLMAN

NOVEMBER 6, 1976
APRIL 22, 2004

Not every man really lives.

NFL Commissioner Paul Tagliabue pays his respects at San Jose memorial service

BAHSTON:
FIRST IN LIBERTY
FIRST IN CREME PIES
SECOND IN THE AMERICAN LEAGUE

Bob Ryan

*Bob Ryan is a Boston Globe columnist and a regular on
ESPN's* The Sports Reporters.

W ars fought many time zones away are
abstracts. They don't become personal until
there is a death in *your* family, or on *your*
block, or in *your* office.

Pat Tillman, 27, was a most unusual and admirable young
man who made news a little less than two years ago by
announcing he was spurning a $3.6 million contract offer
from the Cardinals to join the Army in the hopes of becom-
ing a Ranger. He was joined in this quest by his brother
Kevin, a former minor league baseball player.

The news did, and didn't, surprise people who knew Pat
Tillman. It did because it was an unprecedented act in
the modern sports world. You'd have to go back to
World War II—when the likes of Bob Feller were enlisting on Dec. 8, 1941—to find any remotely comparable
action on the part of a professional sports figure.

But WWII was a very different matter than 9/11, the event that inspired Tillman. War was coming then, and everyone knew it long before Pearl Harbor. America was needed to save Western civilization, and by the end of 1942 it was pretty much unthinkable for an athlete not to get involved. And while sports figures were doing well financially, the gap between what an average baseball player made (baseball being the only sport of true import) and what an average worker made wasn't very significant.

> **He was a challenge guy who impulsively ran a marathon and who trained for the 2001 NFL season by completing a triathlon.**

There was no general call to arms following 9/11, and there was no stampede to the recruiting office on the part of robust young professional athletes. There was no long line of youthful patriots willing to forego millions of dollars to act on a deep personal principle. There was just one such person, and his name was Pat Tillman. And those who knew him weren't surprised, not one bit.

Pat Tillman was *sui generis*. He was a 5-foot-11-inch, 200-pound bundle of muscle and energy who also happened to be a summa cum laude graduate of Arizona State University. As an undergrad, he would occasionally meditate atop a 200-foot light tower hovering over Sun Devil Stadium. He was a challenge guy who impulsively ran a marathon and who trained for the 2001 NFL season by completing a triathlon.

Not for a second did anyone regard him as average. Pat Tillman was, well, Pat Tillman. In that sense, no Tillman decision would ever come as a complete shock.

Here is what Cardinals assistant offensive line coach Mike Devlin said to the Arizona Republic when he heard that Tillman was walking away from $3.6 million in the hopes of becoming an Army Ranger: "I don't think [Tillman's decision] blew anyone away. He marches to a different drummer. When everyone else is trying to relax, he's reading about Zen Buddhism. He was always testing himself, philosophically speaking."

He was politely referred to as an NFL overachiever after advancing from the lowly status of a seventh-round pick to a safety who would set a team record in tackles during the 2000 season. Was he a great player? No. But he was a Belichickian player, a smart, honest, dedicated T-E-A-M player, the kind of guy who would actually give his team the proverbial "hometown discount" when it was time to re-sign when his original contract expired.

Dave McGinnis was his coach at the time, and he was filled with admiration. "Pat's decision was one that was made with honor, integrity, and dignity," McGinnis declared.

Here is perhaps the only other thing you need to know about Patrick Daniel Tillman. He died without publicly explaining himself.

All we know is that his agent, Frank Bauer, says Tillman was "deeply affected" by the events of 9/11.

But that's it. When Pat Tillman announced his decision to quit football and become a soldier, he gave no press conference. He never once granted an interview during his training. When he returned last December after completing a tour of duty in Iraq, he paid a visit to the locker room to renew acquaintances, but he left by a side door before reporters were admitted.

He did speak with McGinnis and the Cardinals' coaching staff, and he did have breakfast with owner Bill Bidwill, in whose box he watched the game. But he did not dish with the press about the whys and wherefores of his decision.

McGinnis did refer to what Tillman had to say as "mesmerizing."

He obviously spoke to his old friends with the understanding that what he had to say was personally classified information. The same was, and is, true of his brother Kevin.

The Tillman brothers were honored, in absentia, with ESPN's Arthur Ashe Courage Award by **ESPN** in July 2003. They were represented by their younger brother Richard, who could express his secondhand thanks.

"They're pleased," said Patrick Tillman, their father, "but they've never done any of this for show."

Clearly, the Tillman way is to embrace a principle and act on it. Pat Tillman was not motivated by fame or fortune, but by a strong sense of honor. He was bright and educated. He had options in life. He was thoughtful and reasoned. He knew what he wanted, and he surely knew the risks his choice entailed.

He had a purpose in life.

What he wasn't, was lucky.

Or maybe he was.

ESPN debuted September 7, 1990. ESPN2 debuted October 1, 1993. *ESPN The Magazine* made its first appearance on March 11, 1998.

We opened our sanctuary after Pat's death for people to come and pray or meditate. People dropped off several types of items and flowers that had been sent to the memorial and to his family. Then, on Sunday, I used Pat's example in my sermon.

In my sermon, I focused on 2 Timothy, Chapter 1, which talks about family, faith and fearlessness. Paul told Timothy, "You know the Scriptures. You've been taught them by your mother and grandmother, and those Scriptures are the ones that have made you the minister that you are." I told the congregation that family has a lot to do with what happens. Almost every one of our gang members has a parent wound or an anger against someone in the family…so family is a big key for all of us. Also, fearlessness. There's a flame, a fire, a desire to be able to do what Pat Tillman did. We're taught that God has not given us a spirit of fear, but rather one of love and power and of sound mind. Pat's fearlessness came from. No matter what happened, God was in charge. So, I focused on those things.

Pat had a great I.Q., with great scores in high school and college, and his brother does as well. I credit the family tremendously for the job that they did raising their boys. Those types of people always flow out of healthy-well-rounded environments. Whoever instilled those values and principles in him did a phenomenal job.

Everyone can learn from Pat's example. In our area, we have our regular church youth, gang members and then adults who may have an attitude of politics in general. I pretty much tell people when they talk about politicians that each politician has an agenda. Every one of them could learn something from Pat Tillman. He didn't have an agenda. He just did what he felt was right.

Every politician should have Pat Tillman's attitude that the cause justifies the risk.

Pat Tillman's story should speak to the youth of America, especially, to say: "Here's a hole that this guy left. You can make a similar difference in people's lives." All of us can raise our standards, our levels. That alone preaches a thousand sermons.

—**DR. JOSEPH CHAVEZ**, pastor, the Phoenix Inner City Church

On a Friday morning, I learned Pat Tillman died in combat in Afghanistan.

Hours later, I wept.

...At Cal Poly, San Luis Obispo, in 2000, I had four roommates in a rundown, rented house near campus. One of those roommates was Pat's brother, Kevin Tillman.

The first visit I remember was Super Bowl weekend. With about 40 people in our house crammed around the TV, Pat bought enough pizza for everyone. Few people knew who paid for them. During the game, there wasn't one time when he referred to playing in the NFL. That night, he slept on our uncomfortable couch and left the next day in his tired white Jeep.

The next time he visited I was able to spent more time with him. Naturally, I was excited to ask him questions about the NFL. He told me about which receivers talked the best trash and how he rarely participated in the on-field banter.

Future visits confirmed what was evident after spending the first five minutes with him. He was genuine. He never felt compelled to make sure everyone knew he played professional football, and he treated everyone with respect. By witnessing interactions with his then fiancée, now a widow, and with Kevin, it was clear how lucky they felt to spend time with Pat.

—**JOE NOLAN**, *Oakland Tribune*

DOWN AT THE CORNER
OF WHAT AND IF

Darren Urban

Darren Urban, 33, covers the Cardinals for the East Valley Tribune, a suburban newspaper outside Phoenix, Arizona

I knew all about Pat Tillman because I went to ASU. I felt like I knew Pat Tillman, the player, when I started to cover him.

The first time it drove home who he was as a player was when he got into a fight with running back Clarence Williams. Clarence was like the nicest person in the world, but in one practice Pat grabbed his shoulder pads and repeatedly gave him knees to the midsection like it was a *Kung Fu* movie. It was a practice, and Pat went full speed in practice. I don't know what Clarence could have done to anger him.

> **...if you needed a quote after the game you went to Tillman because he was so blunt**

I tell you one thing—if you needed a quote after the game you went to Tillman because he was so blunt. As long as you were asking him something about the team he was great, as long as you didn't ask him about himself. He didn't want to talk about himself.

I remember talking to him about a story I was writing on the Cardinals defense. He was really good, saying, "We sucked on defense last year. We need to get better." He's so blunt. I remember talking to him about how nobody showed up at the games. I remember him saying, "Why would anybody want to come to our games? We basically suck." He was a very "I don't give excuses" type of person.

At the end of the 2000 season, the **Cardinals** didn't even look like they gave a crap on the road. They were acting like they didn't care. The score at the end was like 44-10, but what I remember most was Jacksonville scored every time it had the ball except for its last possession. It was a pathetic performance. We reporters went into the locker room, and Pat was the first person you went to after games like that. The question was something along the lines of, "Where do you guys turn?" Pat went off. He said, "Everybody has things to deal with, everybody has injuries, everybody has problems, other teams go through coaching changes. Nobody cares. After awhile you have to stop complaining about the pain and deliver the baby. Around here, we're not showing anybody the baby, we're just bitching about the pain."

> Pat went off....After awhile you have to stop complaining about the pain and deliver the baby.

That's what always struck me about him: He didn't want to accept any excuses. In the end, one of the things that bothered him about some of the guys on the team was that he thought they were skirting through without giving it their all.

The plaza surrounding the Cardinals' new stadium will be named Pat Tillman Freedom Plaza, the team announced. Tillman's No. 40 jersey also will be retired.

The day we found out he was going in the Army was unusual. I had written a story ten days before about the mystery of Pat Tillman, and why he hadn't signed his contract. It made no sense why he hadn't signed his deal yet. One day we get in there to the Cardinals facility, and we're told Mac (coach Dave McGinnis) needs to talk to us, the beat writers, but we can't talk to anybody else. Mac came down, pulled us back in the interview room and closed the door so nobody could hear. At this point, I'm freaking out. He sits up there and says, "Well, I need to talk to you guys about what's happening with Pat Tillman." I'm sure he's about to say Pat Tillman has cancer. He said, "Pat Tillman has decided to join the Army." There was like silence for ten seconds until Mac made fun of my mouth being open. It came so far out of left field that it was just mind-boggling. A couple of days later, Pat came through the team's training facility, and I happened to see him. I said, "You got time for a couple of questions?" He looked at me and smiled and said, "Nope." A little while later, he came through as he was leaving for the last time. I was there with a couple of reporters, and we congratulated him. As he was going out the door, we said, "Hey, if you ever decide to tell your story, don't forget about the local guys." He said, "I really appreciate the offer, but it ain't going to happen." That's the last time I saw his face.

Pat was just Pat. When he went and ran the triathlon, I wasn't surprised. You kind of get that little smile and say, "That's Pat." Anything Pat did, you didn't think

> **I said, "You got time for a couple of questions?" He looked at me and smiled and said, "Nope."**

twice about it. When I think back on it, I got to the training facility about 8 a.m. on September 11, 2001, and even though it was a Tuesday, the players' day off, it did not surprise me that the one player who showed up that day was Pat Tillman. I sat in those big, orange comfy chairs right next to Pat, and we watched for about twenty to thirty minutes on television. We had some general conversation, and, at one point, I asked him a question. He basically said, "As football players, we're nothing, we're worthless, we're actors." Much later on, I began to realize that quote had greater significance than I knew.

Chapter 5

Ranger Down

Mission Accomplicated

ON BRAVE OLD ARMY TEAM

Joseph Bush

Joseph Bush, 22, is a staff sergeant in the 56th Medical Support Group at Luke Air Force Base in Glendale, Arizona. He met Tillman on March 27, 2003, while they were standing in line outside a mini-mart in the Saudi Arabian desert.

I knew who Pat was the minute I saw him. I was a fan of his when he played at ASU. I asked him why he got out of the pros. I said, "Why would you want to do that? I would never think of doing it."

It was so serious. He said he loved his brother, Kevin, who enlisted with Pat, and his country so much he wanted to do it. I'm like, "This dude must really love his country to pass up all that money."

He told me he liked the military life but that it was scary at first. We didn't talk about the war much. We wanted to lighten the mood. He talked about places he had been to. He kept telling me I had to get a Eurorail pass to travel across Europe. He said I had to do that before I die.

I wrote an entry in my journal that day: "Day 19. After a backbreaking day of work at the fallout, me and my buddy, Patterson, went to the new Basic-X and out of nowhere who strolls up behind us? Pat Tillman. We're waiting in line about two hours, just shooting the breeze, and we damn near told each other our life histories. That is really cool. He's in Washington now but on a three-year enlistment. He said, 'When we get out, we're gonna party together in Phoenix.' Man I can't believe this happened here. That dude was one of my favorite players. I gotta tell my old man about this one when I get home."

"Day 29. I ran into Tillman and some of his buddies.

I saw Pat again ten days later and put another log in my journal: "Day 29. I ran into Tillman and some of his buddies. They said they should be heading out about nightfall. I don't envy what they do. I think Pat's a standup guy for putting his butt on the line like that. Imagine passing up millions of dollars just to go fight for your country. This dude is a living legend. They are really cool cats. My prayers are with all of them."

When we were leaving the store, we said we should get together and have a few beers when we got back to Arizona. When I saw on the news that he passed away, I remembered it was almost the same time last year that we were standing next to each other in the middle of the desert. It was unreal!

WAR IS H. E. DOUBLE HOCKEY STICKS

Corwin Brown

Corwin Brown first met Pat Tillman on the football field after a game, while Brown played linebacker at Oregon State. After graduating in the spring of 1998 with a major in history/political science, Brown joined the Army in fall of that year. Today, Brown works for the Colorado Army National Guard.

The first time I saw Pat on the field, here was this little guy doing kick offs and kick-off returns. I thought who is this guy with a mullet? That's what his hair looked like, coming out of his helmet.

When you meet someone, you can tell what type of person he is by how he listens, how he concentrates, and that sort of thing. Pat had that presence about him. We first met after a game, just introducing ourselves to one another. We talked for a few minutes and then headed toward the locker room. He seemed to be cool. Anytime we ran into each other, we talked but it never was anything extensive. Getting to know opponents in football is a little different than other sports because you can't really see the person's face during a game.

Pat was such a fast player. In the college game, bar none, speed kills. I don't care how big you are. If you're fast and can hit hard, you can play. Sure, weight helps, but all that matters is with how much intensity you deliver the package. Pat could deliver just fine.

I joined the Army in the fall of 1998. I planned to go into the Army, work on my Master's and get my commission. Things got pushed back slowly, and it hasn't worked out according to that plan.

I went through Special Forces Assessment Selection (aka 'Selection Process'), just before 9/11. I was in the National Guard, and working on my brokerage license. Once 9/11 hit, all bets were off. The next thing we knew, we were going to war. Most of the guys in my company, probably 70 percent, had been in combat before—Vietnam, Grenada, covert operations here and there, Panama, Somalia, Bosnia—but they all had their own lives. That unit was doing prepping operations in Saudi Arabia long before the war actually started. I was going to go over to the Middle East with the Special Forces unit in September 2002, but I had broken my leg a few months earlier snowboarding and I ended up on Special Operations assignments.

When I heard Pat was leaving the NFL to join the Army, I thought it was gutsy. I could not believe it. When you're a college athlete, especially playing a big sport at a big school, you tend to get a big head. When I joined the military, I quickly learned that playing college football was not real life. The military was real life. All these athletes get paid millions of dollars to play a game. That's it. When you have so much, you have that much more to lose. So I was really impressed when Pat made the move. I wanted to write him a letter to tell him how classy I thought it was.

The 2nd Ranger Battalion is known to have the best physically fit Rangers in Regiment, but all are equal as

Rangers. They have the best test scores, they're the most physically fit, you name it. Most Rangers are pretty smart, pretty alert, because so much is demanded of them. The Rangers are storm troopers. They attack, they get in and get out. Pat was in 2nd Ranger Battalion out of Fort Lewis, A-company. He fit that profile of a Ranger—he had the intelligence, beefy face, beefy, cut body.

Pat also had dedication. It says a lot about a player who's willing to stay home to play, turning down millions of dollars to play somewhere else. Anyone can bounce around. But when Pat stayed in Arizona, instead of going to St. Louis, that said a lot.

I was hoping to see more athletes follow Pat's lead and join the Armed Forces. It doesn't surprise me, though, that they haven't. They love their country but they're not willing to give up millions of dollars to fight for their country. Pat was willing to make that sacrifice.

I've met several former college athletes who joined the military. You get the same type of adrenaline rush depending on what you get into. It's real life, as opposed to fantasy. People look at athletes as if they do something incredible...they play a sport. One of my buddies at work was in 2nd Ranger Battalion, and after Pat's death we started talking about it. He said that we didn't see Pat any differently than any other Ranger.

In my mind, what Pat did is classic. It's worth of all the recognition he's receiving. Leaving the NFL to join the Army took a lot of guts. Most people don't have the guts to give up everything, especially right after getting married. He stepped up for his country and put it ahead of everything else.

ON DUTY AND COMMITMENT

L.A. Chang

L. A. Chang is a writer for the San Jose Mercury News.

Pat Tillman is not my hero. It does not mean I have not thought of him. I have, a lot. Who hasn't thought about the San Jose athlete who abandoned a bright NFL career to enlist in the Army after Sept. 11? Who hasn't thought about him since he was killed in Afghanistan?

Pat Tillman is not my hero. The media made his name a household word. Senator John McCain and California's first lady, Maria Shriver, came to his memorial service in San Jose's Rose Garden. And of course, everyone from **Governor Arnold Schwarzenegger** to sports-talk shock jock Jim Rome called him a hero many times over.

But "hero" is a word of diminished power nowadays. You can be a hero for hitting home runs in major league baseball. In our "hyperpatriotic" atmosphere, you can be a hero for just being in the military. Is that what Pat Tillman did?

I've thought of him a lot in recent days for other things.

I admire deeply his enlistment, his commitment to service to his country. I admire his convictions that led him to do what he did. Without talking about it.

Arnold Schwarzenegger graduated from the University of Wisconsin-Madison in 1979.

In fact, I admire his refusal to talk about it.

This is not something a member of the news media is supposed to say. We want people to talk. We want to create a fuller picture of the man, so that readers or viewers understand who and what was lost. We abhor the vacuum of silence. And too often the news media fills that empty space with speculation.

In Tillman's silence, and his family's silence until the memorial service, they created a space for reflection. On the meaning of heroism, duty, commitment.

So much of American society today is about baring all and getting all. Athletes talk about "taking care of my family" when negotiating multimillion-dollar contracts. Many of us dream of being an American Idol.

Like it or not, our preoccupation with celebrity and with talk reflects what is important to us. Tillman's silence was a statement about something else that should be important to us.

I watched the **"Nightline"** broadcast, during which the names of 721 fallen soldiers from the war in Iraq were read. Their pictures, when possible, were shown, along with their military branch, rank and age. Those who were killed after May 1 were acknowledged but not named because the military had not identified them yet.

I was grateful to be able to watch it. One broadcast station owner withheld the program in several markets,

> *Nightline* is the only prime time TV show named after a sporting term. Nightline is a betting line used in horse racing.

asserting that the reading of 721 names was a polemic against the war. For me, it wasn't.

I saw America in those names and faces that crossed the television screen.

The fallen were mere teenagers, and those the age of Tillman, 27. They were reservists in their forties and career military men in their fifties. They were men and women just out of high school, and young adults with children of their own. They were from American Samoa and Lake Forest, Ill., from Calexico, Calif., and Waterford, Conn.

Names such as Pollard and Smith were announced with Chewongse and Garza. Soldiers named Singh fell in Iraq just like those named Van Dusen.

Tillman's name was not among those read because he served in Afghanistan, that other front that was almost forgotten until his death. Everyone knows *his* name anyway, but not those of the others who have died there.

The fallen were not all heroes. But they all did their duty.

Shriver invoked the famous words of her fallen uncle, President John F. Kennedy: "Ask not what your country can do for you. Ask what you can do for your country."

Once that meant something.

Pat Tillman is not my hero. But he did his duty.

And that means something deeper.

THE ULTIMATE TEAMMATE ON AMERICA'S TEAM

Mark Purdy

Mark Purdy is a highly respected columnist for the San Jose, Mercury News.

Pat Tillman would have hated what has happened. In the space of one morning, he was transformed from one of many brave and tragic battlefield casualties of the war on terror into a singular American icon.

Tillman wanted no part of being an icon. He would have hated that. In fact, he would have hated people writing about him hating that. He wanted to go fight the bad guys of the world because he thought it was the right thing to do for his country. He wasn't looking to become a magazine cover.

Now, he's going to be one. That is what happens when a man gives up what is supposed to be the American dream job—that of a millionaire athlete who is cheered by thousands—and enlists as a soldier who puts his life on the line.

And then loses that life. In combat. While confronting our worst enemy nearly face-to-face.

For that is exactly what Tillman was doing, according to initial reports. He was on patrol with his U.S. Army Rangers unit in Afghanistan, tracking down remnants of the Taliban and al-Qaida. Tillman was killed when his patrol vehicle came under attack.

There is no greater heroism, and I don't care if he would have hated me saying so. Tillman represented the best of us, and he was a San Jose citizen all the way, unpretentious and unimpressed with his celebrity. He was the classic Silicon Valley individualist, an independent thinker with a fearless bent to take risks, and the confidence to pull it off.

> **There is no greater heroism, and I don't care if he would have hated me saying so.**

The difference, of course, is that he wore a football helmet, first at Leland High, then at Arizona State and lastly for the Arizona Cardinals at the highest level of his sport.

And then, in May 2002, he spurned a $3.6 million NFL contract and signed up for a $17,000 per year Army job.

Tillman made it through the elite Rangers training, which only 35 percent of candidates pass. He served in Iraq, took a break, then headed to Afghanistan. It was an extraordinary story, but Tillman wanted no part of helping people tell it. He never publicly explained his decision. He relentlessly refused any interviews on the subject.

Oh, we pursued him. So did other Bay Area newspapers. So did the Arizona media. So did the national television networks.

Tillman resisted, and never wavered. I admired him for his stubbornness. The cynic in me was waiting for Tillman's agent to announce a book deal, or a corporate

Tillman resisted, and never wavered.

tie-in. It didn't happen. I admittedly interviewed Tillman just four or five times, usually quick encounters in locker rooms after games. Still, he was as unique a local sports character as I have encountered.

Barbara Beard, who was the athletic director at Leland High, had it exactly right in 1997 when she gave *Sports Illustrated* this quote about Tillman: "He's driving on the same highway as everybody else, but he's on the other side of the road."

Tillman was not an awesome physical presence, at 5-foot-11 and about 200 pounds. Common scouting wisdom tagged him as a "tweener," someone who was not big and strong enough to play linebacker at the college level, but too small and slow to play safety.

Nevertheless, Arizona State took a chance. The coaches asked him to redshirt as a freshman, meaning he would have sat out a season to gain a fifth year of eligibility. Tillman said they could redshirt him if they wished, but that he was going to finish college in four years and move on.

Tillman kept his promise. He played linebacker for the Sun Devils, helped them reach the 1997 Rose Bowl, then graduated in 3 ½ years. But he never grew the big head. Honest to a fault, Tillman even offered up to one interviewer the information that at Leland, he had been charged with felony assault for beating up a kid who was picking a fight with one of Tillman's friends.

After his 30-day stay in juvenile detention, the charge was reduced to a misdemeanor and the record was sealed. No one would have known about it if Tillman had not gone public with the details. But he had learned from the experience. He wanted people to realize that other kids who get in trouble can learn, too.

I totally understand why Tillman might have cringed at the way his death was glorified. He probably would point out all the other American casualties in this war and say we need to honor them equally. Instead, politicians who never knew him were eulogizing Tillman, saying he "proved there are still heroes in sports."

Wrong. There are no true heroes in sports. There are sportsmen and sportswomen who become heroes. But not very many of them.

If you talked to anyone who played football alongside Tillman, they would tell you he was the ultimate football teammate. And in the end, he was the country's ultimate teammate.

Wherever he is, I hope Tillman doesn't hate me saying that.

ON RARE COURAGE

Senator John McCain

U.S. Sen. John McCain, R-Ariz., has a long career of public service. After graduating from the Naval Academy in 1958, John McCain began his career as a Naval aviator. In 1982, he was elected to Congress representing what was then the first congressional district of Arizona. In 1986, he was elected to the United States Senate to take the place of Arizona's great Senator Barry Goldwater. Senator McCain is currently the senior senator from Arizona.

In 2000, McCain ran unsuccessfully for the Republican nomination for President of the United States. He is currently the Chairman of the Senate Committee on Commerce, Science, and Transportation, and serves on the Armed Services, and Indian Affairs Committees.

I never had the honor of meeting Pat Tillman, and I'm the poorer for it. By all accounts, he was quite a man, and it would have been a great privilege to have called him a friend. He is remembered as a good son, brother and husband, a loyal friend, an excellent student, an over achieving athlete, a decent, considerate person, a solid citizen in every respect. It is obvious to everyone that Pat was raised in a good and loving family to be an honorable man and to have the courage to possess the virtues that make an honorable life.

> **I never had the honor of meeting Pat Tillman, and I'm the poorer for it.**

Many American families have suffered the same terrible sacrifice that the Tillman family now suffers. The courage and patriotism their loved ones exemplified is as fine and compelling as Pat's, and their loss should grieve us just as much. Were he here, I think Pat would insist we cherish their memory and feel their loss no less than his. But it was his uncommon choice of duty to his country over the profession he loved and the riches and other comforts of celebrity, and his humility that make Pat Tillman's life such a welcome lesson in the true meaning of courage and honor.

> **He loved his country, and the values that make us exceptional among nations...**

In our blessed and mostly peaceful society, we're not as familiar with courage as we once were. We ascribe the virtue to all manner of endeavors that only really require skill, fortitude and a little daring, the qualities Pat Tillman showed on the football field. Pat's best service to his country was to remind us all what courage really looks like and that the purpose of all good courage is love.

He loved his country, and the values that make us exceptional among nations, and good. And he worried after the terrible blow we were struck on September 11, 2001, that he had 'never done a damn thing' to serve her. Love and honor oblige us. We are obliged to value our blessings and to pay our debts to those who sacrificed to secure them for us. They are blood debts we owe to the policemen and firemen who raced into the burning towers that others fled; to the men and women who left for dangerous, distant lands to take the war to our enemies and away from us, and to those who fought in all the wars of our history.

Pat Tillman understood his obligations, no better than his comrades in arms, perhaps, but better than many of his contemporaries. He must have known that such debts are not a burden but that their recompense earns us our happiness. So he volunteered to take his place in the ranks and defend his country in a time of peril.

Our country's security doesn't depend on the heroism of every citizen. Nor does our individual happiness depend upon proving ourselves heroic. But we have to be worthy of the sacrifices made on our behalf. We have to love our freedom, not just for the ease or material benefits it provides, not just for the autonomy it guarantees us, but for the goodness it makes possible. We have to love it so much we won't let it be constrained by fear or selfishness. We have to love it as much, even if not as heroically, as Pat Tillman loved it.

It would be false to pretend that Pat's death hasn't hurt us. The loss of every fallen soldier should hurt us lest we ever forget the terrible costs of war and the sublime love of those who sacrifice everything on our behalf. I respect and mourn his death. But I will not dwell on the grief it occasioned when in better days I remember what he did for us. I will remember that Pat Tillman was an Army Ranger. He served one combat tour in Iraq and had begun another in Afghanistan where he was killed. I will remember that his family and his country lost a good man. But I will also remember that while many of us may be blessed to live a longer life than he did, few of us will ever live a better one. And I will celebrate and encourage my children to celebrate the brief, brave and happy life of Pat Tillman, a most honorable man.

The first mission we conducted, there was a whole lot of fire coming in. There were casualties right off the bat and one happened to be a Ranger we were working with. He was the primary saw-gunner, which is a light machine gun, carried by one man. He was in Pat's platoon. He got shot right off the bat. Pat, who was the secondary gunner, now became the No. 1 slot, and for the duration, was the No. 1 guy doing every single mission after that. He was thirsty to be the best. He wanted to be the best saw-gunner. He wanted to get every piece of information that he possibly could from my guys and his guys. He couldn't get enough. Take it from me – there is nothing better than having a bunch of squared-away Rangers on your side. Pat definitely raised the bar for himself and for his guys – no doubt about it.

If you're a victim of an ambush, there are very few things you can do to increase your chances of survival, but one is to get off that ambush point as fast as you can. One of the vehicles in Pat's convoy could not get off. He made the call. He dismounted his troops, taking the fight to the enemy, uphill, to seize the tactical high ground from the enemy. This gave his brothers in the downed vehicle time to move off that target. He directly saved their lives with that move. Pat sacrificed himself so his brothers could live."

—STEVE WHITE, Navy Seals Chief Petty Officer

THERE'S MORE TO COACHING THAN IGNORING YOUR BEST PLAYER

Skip Bayless

Skip Bayless is a nationally known and respected writer for the San Jose Mercury News. *He previously wrote for the* Dallas Morning News *and the* Chicago Tribune. *His sage comments are often heard on KNBR in San Francisco and on ESPN.*

Six years ago, he was a last-round, what-the-heck draft pick by a bad team looking for a little positive publicity.

Now, of course, the men who were involved in choosing Pat Tillman for the Arizona Cardinals say they saw "something special" in him. But those are just the kind of image-building, crowd-pleasing exaggerations that Tillman despised about professional sports in America.

No, Arizona's personnel department and coaching staff had no idea what made Tillman tick or they would have taken him much earlier. Tillman was the third of their four seventh-round picks in 1998. He was the 226th player selected, only 15 slots from the end.

The Cardinals took this too-small, too-slow linebacker largely because he attended Arizona State, which surrounds their Sun Devil Stadium. Though Tillman did not have the scout-wowing "measurables," he had been named the Pacific-10 Conference's defensive player of the year. What the heck, if he managed to make the team covering punts and kickoffs, maybe a few more ASU fans or students would buy some of the many tickets available for Cardinals games.

Coach Dave McGinnis did have the foresight to move Tillman to safety. But McGinnis could not have known until he witnessed it that Tillman had the one untestable trait rarely seen on a pro football field: utter disregard for his body and that of his opponent.

McGinnis did have the foresight to move Tillman to safety. You see big hitters in college who lose some of their nerve against bigger, stronger, meaner NFL players. You see NFL "tough guys" occasionally flinch. But Tillman's fearlessness went beyond the typical NFL warrior mentality.

At 5-foot-11 and 202 pounds, Tillman would launch himself into oncoming freight trains—ball-carriers, pulling guards, tight ends—with a Marine-like give-yourself-up-for-dead abandon rarely seen beyond an actual field of battle. Tillman scared other NFL players. If he had been a little faster and more athletic, he would have been the next Ronnie Lott. Lott scared people, too. But Lott is in the Hall of Fame.

Tillman never set out to be decorated for his football valor. Leading the Cardinals in tackles one season was not a big deal to him because it didn't really push him to his physical or mental limits. He loved rock-climbing because one mistake could be fatal. Heck, in college he used to climb to the top of the stadium's 200-foot light standards just to meditate.

Knocking down bigger football players didn't impress Tillman nearly as much as it did us.

Some players chosen in the late rounds in this year's NFL draft will beat the odds because scouts misjudged their knack for making plays with their mind or vision or instincts or hands or immeasurable in-game quickness. But a few players with limited ability—a very few —make it because they are as brave as the men who kept this country free during the wars of the 20th century.

In a way, the NFL was child's play to a young man from San Jose.

"He wanted the real thing," said another Pat T., this one Toomay, the former Raiders defensive end who is now a novelist and a contributor to ESPN.com. Toomay, the son of an Air Force general, grew up on bases being taught the military mindset.

> ...the NFL was child's play to a young man from San Jose.

Toomay said: "In football, you don't get killed. You can get maimed, but not killed. But you could see in Tillman's pictures from the time he was in college that he had this knowing look—a look of determination and resignation. He knew where he was going. It was haunting, really.

"It's the look of the military warrior. It borders on the spiritual. It's as if you're born to lay it on the line for the mission. It's what you are."

Tillman did not choose to join the Army as much as his destiny chose him. It was not hard for him to walk away from a three-year, $3.6 million contract offer because fame and fortune disgusted him. Making him watch ESPN's draft coverage would have been torture. The blood-sucking agents mugging for the cameras, the family and "friends" mobbing the suddenly rich first-round picks, the Manning family intimidating San Diego into working out a deal so that Eli can play in New York—it all seemed so trivial to him after Sept. 11.

Yet, in the biggest picture, it all seemed so dear.

On the Cardinals' Web site are words Tillman spoke soon after the twin towers fell: "You don't realize how great a life we have…That life wasn't built overnight…A lot of my family has gone and fought in wars and I haven't really done a damn thing as far as laying myself on the line."

> **Thank God this country has had so many Pat Tillmans to protect it. Here was a man.**

This was not some agent-inspired stunt. Tillman did not want to return triumphantly to become TV's next Geraldo Rivera or radio's next Oliver North. No, he told his family and friends not to talk to the media about him and his brother, both of whom tried to beat the odds and become members of the elite 75th Ranger Regiment. Only about 35 percent make it. They did.

Please, this is not to suggest Tillman wanted to die. But surely few men have died a more satisfying death. He and his brother were on a mission battling Taliban and Al-Qaida forces in Afghanistan. Presumably, they were hunting for Osama bin Laden.

In a way, this was what Tillman was born to do. Few if any of the newest NFL draftees can begin to comprehend or appreciate that. But true heroes like Tillman have made their only-in-America fame and fortune possible.

Thank God this country has had so many Pat Tillmans to protect it. Here was a man.

On April 22, 2004, Pat Tillman graduated life with honors and no regrets.